Create Your Health Naturally

– FREDA GAISIE –

An environmentally friendly book printed and bound in England by
www.printondemand-worldwide.com

Mixed Sources
Product group from well-managed
forests, and other controlled sources
www.fsc.org Cert no. TT-COC-002641
© 1996 Forest Stewardship Council
FSC

PEFC Certified
This product is
from sustainably
managed forests
and controlled
sources
www.pefc.org
PEFC
PEFC/16-33-415

This book is made entirely of chain-of-custody materials

http://www.fast-print.net/bookshop

CREATE YOUR HEALTH NATURALLY
Copyright © Freda Gaisie 2015

A catalogue record for this book is available from the British Library

ISBN 978-178456-271-7

First published 2015 by
FASTPRINT PUBLISHING
Peterborough, England.

Preface

I got to a point in my life where I said to myself, I can't take this pain anymore. I know there's an answer, I just need to find it. After years of debilitating pain and constant hospitalisation, I began to search for a way out of my misery. I refused to give up and I eventually found the answers to live a pain-free and disease free life. The reason I wrote this book is that I know there are countless others that are in the same position as I was, and I believe this book will help immensely. Although it has taken quite a few years of research, studies, courses and personal experience, the timing is now right, and with the upsurge of minor and chronic conditions increasing at an alarming rate, it's important to know that there are many options available to you to take control of your own health and heal yourself naturally. There are many paths to health, but it's about finding the best path and solution for what you're currently going through. I believe this book will make it so much easier for you to begin your healing journey and it's not as difficult as you may think. Although some of the information is basic knowledge based on common sense information, the majority are unaware of it and continue to suffer and even die prematurely. I have repeated some important facts, just to get across the urgency of the matter, plus we remember when we hear something over again.

You will learn the simple protocol that helped me put my body in the perfect state to begin the healing process.

I have learnt from some amazing mentors who believe that there are no incurable diseases, and their knowledge and teachings have been instrumental in the writing of this book

"Modern man has made many advancements, but because man can be selfish by nature, these advancements are often first and foremost about making more profit, even when it comes to our food and ultimately our health. We can send a man to the moon and back, but in terms of our health, we are sicker than we have ever been. What is going on? It seems that we were doing far better in the past when we completely relied on Mother Nature for our sustenance, thus this is where we need to return to, if we are to see a complete reversal and restoration of the health of the nations." Create your health through Mother Nature where life and health is abundant.

~Freda Gaisie~
Natural health consultant, raw food/vegan chef and natural health advocate and coach.

This book has been written and compiled through extensive research over the last ten years, together with my own insights and experiences and the experiences of others who have also healed themselves naturally. The idea to write this book came about five years ago when I got fed up of hearing and seeing so many people around me getting sick and even dying. So I decided to do something about it by writing this book. The only thing I ask is that you are open-minded as you are reading.

Foreword

A cliché I know "health is wealth" and this will be understood more, as the book you hold in your hands contains some interesting information on the discovery of making your health a priority.

Having experienced a variety of on-going health concerns for many years Freda has made it her lifelong mission to heal herself by using natural remedies and changing her diet and life style and she has written this book "Create Your Health" to encourage others who have health challenges and who are looking for answers and solutions to turn their health around too.

I have been touched by her determination and belief and feel honoured that Freda has asked me to write the forward to this book that I consider will help others discover and find ways to get their health back on track. This book will help you understand and implement and prepare healthy recipes that make you feel energised and more alive than you have ever done before by using natural raw ingredients free from chemicals and preservatives of which research and facts have proved to be causing so many common ailments and disease found in society today. Humans have been moving away from real food for many years because of life style, economy and convenience as we end up using more food products, some that don't even have a trace of real food that continues to contribute to poor health. As Freda states in her book most of the food we eat is dead food and over cooked. I know when I eat real fresh raw food I feel so much better, much lighter and full of energy.

To eliminate many diseases and ailments we need to start looking at what nutrition our bodies need rather than what we want to feed it. In Freda's book Create Your Health she helps you to make those choices by providing mouth-watering recipes, tools and the know how in doing this.

We are living longer but have never been sicker than we are now. Living to be old and decrepit or living to old and full of energy is a choice and by reading Freda's book you will begin to understand that.

Besides good nutrition one must be both physically and mentally active; they all go hand in hand.
Freda has written this book in a simple and easy way to understand for anyone who wants to create their own health and experience longevity.

Freda is a great friend who I have known for many years and she is a constant source of information and knowledge and continually supports people in the direction of empowerment so they can help themselves. At the end of the day the choice is yours if you want to make the changes the help and support is there.
Freda has turned her health around. I remember the days when she used to have the most terrible crisis when her body used to break down with so much pain and today she is pain free and happy because she created this for herself without relying on anyone else to do it for her, she found the answers for herself.
I encourage you to read this book and then apply the changes to your diet and lifestyle when you change things you will be experiencing a whole new you changing in front of you.
Thank you Freda, for allowing me to say a few words in this book of which I know will be a gift to many.

~ Kathryn Bami Heather ~

Table of Contents

Dedications

To my beautiful Angelic baby boy, Elyon Elisha Tilki, who never had the chance to see the world as his life slipped away at 8 months in the womb.

To my wonderful mother Emelia Gaisie, whose life was cut short at age 67 due to sickness.

To my amazing nephew, Alexander Gaisie-Walker A brilliant architect, whose life was cut short at only 28 years of age.

To all the members of my family and friends who have lost their lives through sickness.

Acknowledgements

I am so grateful to my creator that after many years of sickness and pain, I was finally lead to discover for myself, true knowledge to the path of healing and great health, energy in abundance and a disease free life. I feel blessed to share the knowledge and experiences I have gained along the way to encourage and show others how they too can help themselves and take responsibility and control over their own health.

To Angela Alexis — whose classes and teachings on natural health and raw foods opened my eyes and motivated me to learn more about how the human body works with food and how the wrong (dead) foods are literally killing us, and living foods that bring health and life to our body.

To Dr Johnson — whose teachings on certain identified common but dangerous foods and cleansing the body, confirmed everything I had learnt about dead foods that affect our body and health in a negative way.

To Dr Sebi — whose teachings on cleansing and electric foods confirmed to me that your body is capable of healing any disease no matter the so-called name and that there are no incurable diseases.

To my family and friends who have been a great support and inspiration to me.

Introduction

I have discovered that sickness is not a mystery as some may think, neither is it complicated and most diseases are reversible.

This statement may come as a surprise to some of you if you have what is so-called an incurable condition, but stay with me on this, it will be explained. One thing we all have in common today is that we all know of, or have heard of someone who's had their life cut short due to sickness, or as I like to call it, one of the "common chronic conditions" of today we see increasing at an alarming rate each year. This has become the norm due to lack of the correct knowledge, but it should be unacceptable to have to live with a chronic condition for the rest of our life or see our family members or friends suffering and dying around us because of a chronic condition that could have been prevented or reversed if only they had the correct information and knowledge to help themselves.

Having spent a large portion of my life sick and in hospitals, I never imagined writing a book on health and healing, but having discovered many truths as well as misinformation around this subject and discovered how we can heal ourselves, I would consider it a tragic waste not to share it with others. I am not an expert by any means, I have merely learnt through my many years of suffering from sickness to research and heal myself naturally, using simple basic natural methods of nature and believe the information in this book can save lives if applied.

I constantly encourage others to do their own research, as there is a lot of good and helpful information out there amongst the misinformation and a lot of hidden truths to discover. But the misinformation is making and keeping people sick.

"The truth will set you free from sickness"

Some of what I will be sharing in this book may be new to some of you or may even come as a surprise, but most of the information is based on common sense, simplicity and going back to Mother Nature. The biggest problem that people have concerning sickness and disease is lack of knowledge because we have been raised in a society that has trained us to put our health in the hands of others. The truth for you is "that which works for you."

Statistics have shown that the common chronic conditions of today are nutritionally and toxin-related and 80% of people in the US and UK will die prematurely as a result of their diet. Those statistics are far too high for us not to be active in taking preventive measures.

Our body is also out of balance for this same reason and the lacking of natural fuel (nutrition) that is essential for the running and maintenance of the body are missing.

Ignorance is not bliss

I have heard that ignorance is bliss, but that could not be further from the truth. We have also heard that knowledge is power, but true knowledge and applied knowledge is more powerful as it gets results. If you've been doing something for a long time and are not seeing any results, then it's more likely to be false information or you need to try something else because it's not working for you.

Real and true knowledge starts by studying and research rather than just believing what you're told, especially when you see no change but continue to accept and remain in the same condition because you have been told that your situation is hopeless, and there is nothing else that can be done for you except to live on drugs or just wait to die in six or twelve months, or however long they give you. Don't take my word or anybody's word as final. Please do your own research and help yourself today!

There is always something you can do. There is an answer to every question, but unless you discover that answer for yourself, you will be living in ignorance and ignorance can be very costly, even to the point of cutting one's life short. Ignorance is not bliss as some may think.

Based on the material I have studied from top natural health doctors who are curing people every day, I come from the perspective that has shown me that there are no incurable diseases and there is a cure for every disease known to man, but unless you believe that you can be cured and discover the answer, in your mind, your condition will always remain incurable because of what someone else or a system has told you.

When you're first told that you have an incurable condition, FEAR grips you, and in that fearful state, people generally accept and live with it and do what they're told even if it means taking a cocktail of drugs each day because you depend on those you think should know best. Always get a second or even third opinion. I recently read an article from a well-known doctor in the US, talking about the amount false diagnosis of patients with a condition they did not have, just to make more profit.

I have medical doctors in my family as well as friends that are doctors who are very sincere and genuinely want to help their patients, but I discovered that within the seven or so years of study that a doctor must undergo, they do about two hours of nutritional studies in all that time, and when you consider that nutrition is the basis of a good health, it just does not make any sense.

Although many doctors are sincere and genuinely want to help people, unfortunately they have to go by the book which is based on treating the symptoms rather than the cause, and this can never bring proper healing to the body.

Once you find what is causing the condition, then you know how to treat the cause.

There is plenty that you can do about your condition yourself. Never give up. Continue searching, and you will always find the real answers that can completely change your life. For true results, always start by going back to the basics. I can testify of this with my own health, which I will share with you soon.

You may be surprised to know that people with chronic conditions who refuse to take what they are being told for an answer and do their own research, are finding their own cures for Cancer, Aids, Heart Disease, Diabetes, Asthma, Sickle Cell, you name it. In truth, the real cure comes from your own body when given the correct building blocks to heal itself.

Whatever you have been told there is no cure for, it is possible to find a cure, this may even apply to some of the conditions you may have been born with, all through doing various tests to pinpoint the cause, that is the first thing, then finding what works for you to treat the cause. There is no point trying to treat your symptoms when you do not know the root cause of your condition, you may actually make things worse.

You will benefit greatly by going to a good holistic naturopath with a facility for doing different tests such as toxicity and deficiency tests to try and pinpoint exactly what is causing your condition, then they can advise you exactly how to tackle the causative factor. Which is usually to do with toxicity and deficiency.

If this is the case, it would be good practice for them to start you on a cleansing program to deep cleanse your body, a change of diet and lifestyle, oxygenating the body and other various healing modalities as well as the correct nutrition.

But unless you put yourself in an environment of educating yourself, surrounding yourself with like-minded people and learning as much as you can, you will never know that you can be cured of your condition too and will probably have to live with it for the rest of your life or until it cuts your life short, which is now happening daily and considered normal. People are dying far too young, unnecessarily.

You do not have to be a prisoner of your condition. You can set yourself free whenever you choose to. Why not start today?

CHAPTER 1

Why are so many people getting sick?

We are living in a time where there is an epidemic of sickness. This book addresses the question — why are so many people getting sick and dying and what can you do to prolong your life or prevent it from happening to you? You will see the simple reasons why, and simple solutions to begin your healing journey. You will also see that you do not have to accept your condition or live with it any longer. We will be looking mainly at the number one reason, which is linked to our food. You will also see how foods can cure as well as kill.

There are three main causes of diet related sickness. **Accumulation** of waste in the body, lack of proper blood **Circulation** and **Deficiency** of essential vitamins, minerals, amino acids and nutrients.

We will elaborate on this later. The original design for our body and health is that we may be well and live in optimum health all the days of our life. This was the original design and capabilities of the human body before being forced to live in a man-made toxic environment. Our body was not originally made to break down so easily.

There are various ways in nature that have been made available for us to stay well and healthy. The two main one's are cleansing of the body and through nutrition from our food and observing the natural laws of nature, by eating electric foods that are oxygen rich and contain living enzymes along with the correct minerals and nutrients made available to us by Mother Nature, rather than man-made processed foods that contain a cocktail of chemicals and toxic ingredients that are highly acidic and damaging to the body, the body cannot deal with this onslaught for too long.

The correct fuel for cleansing and nourishing the human body is natural living whole foods such as fruits, vegetables, nuts, seeds, healthy oils and herbs as well as unpolluted oxygen and a natural source of clean living water that were created for our body for fuel, helping our bodies to function correctly, just like a car needs the right fuel to function correctly. We are having health problems because our foods are not what they use to be; even fruits and vegetables have been compromised in some way.

Our ancestors ate real living foods off the land, drank clean living water and lived in an oxygen-rich environment. These were the correct fuel that were originally made available to humanity before the invention of corporate agriculture that began to create toxic processed dead foods that are not found in nature and because of their toxic content, are causing an epidemic of chronic conditions all over the world. The correct foods should grow on trees, below the ground or above the ground, mineral rich and free of chemicals. The best foods for healing our body are not man-made in a factory but come from natural plants that are nourishing and healing to the body. Mother Nature is far superior and advanced in the foods and correct fuel she created for our body, and we can never match this in the attempt of creating dead fake foods that please only our pallet and the wallet of the manufacturers.

The majority have chosen not to stick to the specified foods offered by Mother Nature; this is because of a lack of knowledge or what our environment and those around us have dictated to us because of their lack of knowledge. We please the pallet and eat what we like, not realising what we are truly eating, but having to face the consequences later. We have come so far from the natural living mineral oxygenated and enzyme rich healing foods and the miracle healing benefits of herbs, such as Moringa Oleifera, which is known as the miracle tree, Hemp seeds, Dandelion and many other miraculous healing herbs.

Unfortunately, people with a vested interest have made sickness a mystery, complicated and incurable because there is no profit in curing disease.

Before the establishment of governmental health institutions, people healed themselves naturally through herbs that worked very well for healing all sorts of ailments without the side effects. Some of our native relatives like the Hunza tribe and other tribes in Africa and around the world, who still practice this natural method of living and observing the natural laws of nature, do not know what it is to have cancer, heart disease, diabetes or any other ailments or diseases. They are disease free, and this way of living still works perfectly well for them; the challenge for such groups is in trying to prevent their food and environment from being contaminated and polluted by other nations around the world, which have contaminated their food and polluted their own environment.

You will not find any modern diseases amongst these people because they do not eat the modern western diet. We have heard of cultures that were completely disease free until the western diet was introduced to them, and then they began to get sick with the same chronic diseases. Living in our modern day of new foods and a restaurant culture, comes at a price to our health. We should enjoy our foods and eating out, but just know what you're eating, it's not just about what you eat, but also what you cleanse out of your body.

Since the establishment of government institutions such as local doctors, hospitals and the pharmaceutical industry, people have been trained to automatically put all responsibility for their health and the health of their family completely in the hands of their doctor; the government and modern medicine and have become estranged from the herbs that their ancestors once used successfully in treating everything.

There are many healing herbs all around us, even in our front and back gardens that we think are just weeds, the yellow dandelion, for example is full of nutrients such as calcium, potassium, zinc and vitamins A, B, C and D and offers incredible benefits to many parts of the body. If we knew what sort of benefits could be attained from these plants without any side effects, we would not have to rely on prescription drugs that cannot heal, but only mask the symptoms of the condition.

Most have noticed that they are not getting any better regardless of the amount of medication they are prescribed, but rather getting worse with additional health problems from the side effects of the drugs; then they are prescribed more drugs to counteract the side effects of the first drug, making the body even more toxic. In an emergency, we may need drugs and certainly painkillers, but drugs and painkillers should not be your indefinite normal daily routine, and it does not have to be. There is another way out that gets real results.

To make sure we're not statistics of a chronic condition in the first place, we have to first take responsibility and control for our own health and the health of our family, this begins with true knowledge, educating or even re-educating ourselves through our own research and experiences and seeing what works best for us.

Often we go around in life searching for answers, not realising that what we have been searching for could be right in front of us.

16

When it comes to sickness, we do not believe that it can be that simple to overcome, because you may have been told that what you are facing is incurable and can only be managed with drugs and to keep you as comfortable as possible. I've been there; I know what I'm talking about, but I managed to get myself out of that belief system and deadly trap of being on medication for the rest of my life.

I often say, "Man is a master of complications." Since the establishment of modern medicine, sickness has become big business and so complicated that most people believe that there is no cure for the common chronic conditions or modern diseases of today linked to our foods and toxins.

When the doctor tells you that your condition is incurable, you believe it.

What reason would you have not to? They are seen as authority figures and because the system has been created in such a way to make us dependent on the established systems rather than do our own research to find out why this happened in the first place.

The majority of people will never bother to do their own research because they cannot see beyond the establishment of modern medicine, operations and medication, thinking that it's their only choice. You will be surprised to know that there is a great deal of information available to you that will expand your vision and open your eyes to the truth that you can create your own health and heal yourself naturally.

Before you engage in a new protocol, especially if you have a condition, seek help from a naturopath or someone that understands how the body works with nutrition and deals with toxins and will be able to monitor you along the way.

"Give the body what it needs and the body will heal itself naturally"

I am saddened as I travel around and see tired-looking people queuing up in food outlets to buy dead foods and drinks to put in their already tired bodies. These dead foods slowly poison their entire system making them even more tired and sick. They are probably not aware of the studies that show more than half of the people who die each year are from diet-related illnesses, a result of what they continue to eat and drink on a daily basis, even with foods that are touted as healthy, as well as other toxins they may be breathing in, applying to their body or using in their homes.

This is a good reason to research what you're putting in and on your body. Because something says healthy or natural on the label, it does not mean it is. Checking the ingredients and educate yourself by researching to see what the ingredients actually are, will prevent you from adding more damaging toxic ingredients to your body.

People are led by advertisements and a microwave culture to grab the quickest and easiest solution for food, which is usually dead foods, foods that are not real and contain no nutritional value, assuming that if it's for sale, it must be good for them, and also because of time or lack of knowledge, not taking much notice of what it's slowly doing to their body over a period of time until it finally catches up with them with some type of condition.

People assume that if the food is available to buy then it must be safe to eat. Unfortunately, sooner or later, unaware of what is happening, they will start to feel the results from what they are consuming, when their energy begins to deplete because their cells are starved of nutrition and oxygen, creating an acidic inflamed environment from the dead foods and drinks, a build-up of accumulated toxic waste and lack of proper blood circulation, reducing essential blood supply to different parts of the body. They normally do not associate this with the dead foods they are eating so continue down this path.

Their bodies become deficient of essential life-giving nutrition and oxygen; they begin to get unexplained symptoms such as headaches, tiredness, mood swings etc., they become constipated, their skin may begin to look bad and start to age prematurely. They may develop allergies, their immune systems become depleted, their organs begin to fail, they are labelled with some chronic condition and may be subjected to invasive operations and put on drugs for the rest of their lives or until their body gives up due to the toxic overload in the body.

They may even suffer premature death because the toxic condition was not seen early enough or the drugs they were taking could not treat the root cause but rather caused an adverse reaction in their body.

This grim picture I have painted is real life as we see it today because of the modern lifeless foods and the sickness industry that brings no real solutions because it's about more profits and not your health, but this does not have to be your life or direction if you decide to make the right decisions and choices today. Your diet choices and decisions today will create for your body what you instruct it to create.

In other words, what you consume today can set you up for life and great health or sickness and premature death for the future.

This is not to condemn anybody, my desire is that this book will bring awareness, not fear but hope, and out of love and compassion for people whom I see dying or suffering needlessly every day from minor ailments to chronic diseases that could be brought under control if only they knew how. The condemnation would rather be towards some of the unnecessary and openly toxic substances that are allowed to be added to our foods that we need to look out for and have very little or no control over.

Nevertheless, there is something you can do about it. The only one that can look out for your health is you. Therefore, you must take control by reading labels and asking questions rather than spending money on toxic substances unaware, especially when they do not feed you but can harm you. Vote with your wallet and don't pay to poison yourself, these toxic lifeless foods and products would not be for sale if people were not buying it. Avoiding these will help you in the prevention and elimination of sickness and premature death from substances in your foods and toxins you may be ingesting that are causing some of these chronic conditions that did not exist in the past.

"What you don't know may be killing you," and that's exactly what I'm hoping to get across in this book.

But before you finish reading this book, you will know what to look out for and what to avoid. But you have to be open to learning and educating or even re-educating yourself rather than just going with what you're told or what you see in advertisements. Advertising campaigns are not to benefit you, they are first and foremost to get your money, the whole marketing and design plan is to tempt and lure you into buying and eating their products, but it's not real food, it's mainly lifeless man-made artificial foods that have been created to taste good but contain numerous amounts of toxins and artificial sugars with zero nutrition.

The amount of sugar hidden in these foods that the average person eats is about 20 teaspoons or more per day and sugar is one of the biggest culprits killing us. Showing people a healthier way of eating or taking care of themselves by exposing what they are actually putting in their bodies does not always go down well with some, some simply do not believe it because they think that the government is looking out for them through regulations and also because these dead foods are so addictive and very difficult to give up.

Some simply want to continue with what they have gotten used to regardless of the consequences. I do not blame them because this is the extent of their knowledge, and they are not willing to change. The main thing is that we all have a choice, but it's better to have an informed choice.

In my opinion, these toxic artificial processed foods can honestly be put in the same category as cigarette or drug addiction because you get hooked and get cravings in the same way so it's difficult to give up.

All nations that eat dead toxic foods have to deal with this problem of chronic disease, some more than others. When we look at native cultures that have an average lifespan of well over 100 years without sickness and are still healthy and energetic and in some cases still having children, these are cultures that are living off the land as intended and eat natural living foods, (the original diet for mankind) every day of their lives.

Even if some of these cultures eat animal products, they are not filled with toxins or growth hormones that will affect their body. They engage in periodic cleansing practices of their internal organs such as colon cleansing and cleansing of the organs using herbs and cleansing foods. They have no hereditary conditions either. We have a lot to learn from them.

Most of the time all it takes to get your health back is as simple as changing your diet and start eating real living foods, cleansing your internal organs of accumulated waste from all the dead foods you have been consuming most or all of your life and allowing the body to heal itself. Good nutrition does not come automatically in our modern system, you need to be active in making sure you and your family get the nutrition you need to keep the body well, free of sickness and alive. Again this all comes with looking at labels and research.

The majority of people I meet nowadays are sick or suffering from some health complaint or another that has become an accepted normal part of their lives.
There is a fear of Cancer, Heart Disease, Diabetes, Alzheimer's etc., and even children are now suffering from common degenerative conditions normally seen mainly in the older generation. There is an acceleration of these conditions that can affect anybody regardless of age. Nevertheless, as I mentioned before, it is not a mystery. You can start helping yourself by going back to nature and eating as naturally as you can. If you cannot grow your own food, then support your local organic farmer and buy seasonally from small farmers rather than corporate giants who are more interested in your money more than your health.

In business circles, there is a quote that says, "Only a madman continues to do the same thing and expects a change." If you're sick and continue to do the same thing, you can expect the same results with your life remaining the same. If you're looking for change, you need to change how you're doing things.
The problem is we rarely think about our health until we get sick, maybe because we do not think that it's going to happen to us, and when it does, we wonder how this happened to us. Then we end up in the cycle of having to take tablets, which often promotes further problems down the line, hoping that they will heal us, but tablets cannot heal, they only put a plaster on the symptoms. We all know that prevention is better than a cure. But we do not need to go around fearing that we may get sick someday as sickness can also be manifested through fear, stress and negative thinking; it's about information, applied knowledge and prevention.

Don't leave your health to chance. Learn about what you need to do now, for prevention.

I spent most of my childhood, teenage years and young adult life in and out of hospital beds; the hospital was literally my second home. But all they could do for me was to give me drips for hydration, more oxygen, painkillers to numb the pain and penicillin to prevent me from getting infections that I was susceptible to due to my condition and to keep me as comfortable as possible.

Fifty-three years ago I was born with a hereditary blood disorder called sickle cell anaemia. This causes the shape of the red blood cells to deform into a sickle shape rather than the normal oval shape, restricting oxygen and blood flow, so causing a further lack of oxygen to the body and cells and prevents the blood from circulating properly, so when the cells pass through the small blood vessels they can get stuck, causing extreme and excruciating pains in the joints.

About 25 years ago, I was told by my consultant that people with sickle cell anaemia do not often live beyond the age of 30 years, and he was accurate with that statement because not a lot was known about it back then, and I don't think much is known about it today, so according to those statistics, I only had a few years to live. I have personally known people with sickle cell that have died before the age of 30.

My own nephew, my cousin's son died at the age of 18 because of a sickle cell related condition. I am well past the age of 30 and still living thank God and the fact that I know what to give my body to keep me well, out of hospital and the doctor's office, free of sickness and alive. They are surprised they don't see me anymore. I used to be one of their best customers.

People with sickle cell are routinely put on penicillin and other tablets for the rest of their lives so as to prevent infections.

In my past life, I was admitted to hospital for 2-3 weeks at a time and at least 4-6 times a year dealing with health issues that were as a result of the condition and with horrendous pain. You would not imagine that such pain could exist; it was so bad that I often wished that someone would end my life. Some of my health issues that manifested as a result of the condition in the past, were:

- Sickle cell crisis (Excruciating pains in my joints)
- Constant general aches and pains in my body every day
- Lack of blood circulation, cold hands and feet
- Lack of oxygen through my body
- Two DVTs (blood clots in the leg)
- Laser treatment to seal a hole in my retina
- Retinal detachment (causing damage and a blur to one eye)
- Haemorrhage in the eye
- Floaters in eyes
- Cataract
- Gallstone
- Fibroids
- Partial hearing in one ear
- Hypo splenic (under developed spleen, being susceptible to pneumonia and bacterial infections)
- Pneumonia several times
- Low immune function
- Protein S deficient (risk of thrombosis) blood clots
- Numerous Chest infections
- Numerous Stomach infections
- Cysts in breast
- Pleurisy
- Constant colds and flu
- Lack of energy and shortness of breath

I did not consume the best diet at the time either, I was chronically constipated from childhood not knowing that accumulation of waste in my body and nutritional deficiency was not helping my condition but rather making it worse.

I ate my fair share of fake dead junk foods and drank poisonous fizzy drinks until it was coming out of my nostrils, not realising that I was poisoning my body and contributing to the worsening of my condition by eating these dead foods deficient of the nutrition and oxygen that my body so needed to heal me and keep me healthy and alive.

If I had not been searching for answers, especially after my mother passed away in February 2003, I would never have discovered the correct way of eating and know I probably would be dead by now.

In one of my most painful crisis I ever experienced, the pain was so bad that I could do nothing but scream out. I actually felt myself slipping deeper and deeper away after a while, but I forced myself out of it. I had a destiny like we all do, and I was not about to go anywhere at such a young age. I have since found my purpose in helping others before my life could be cut short by this debilitating condition.

In the year 2000, I started to become more health conscious and became responsible for the foods that I was eating and saw some good improvements, although not yet 100%, I felt much better and healthier.

After my mother passed away in 2003 from a brain haemorrhage leading on from a stroke, it was time for me to make even bigger changes to my diet and health. Even without having the knowledge that I have today, back then, I knew at the time that the numerous amounts of tablets they had prescribed for my mother were in fact making her worse.

I was very concerned for her but did not have the information at that time to help her. When I went to the hospital on the day which was to be her last, I realised they had given her no fluids for quite some time. She was completed dehydrated, could not respond and shortly drifted into a coma. I tried frantically to get the nurses to do something, but nothing was done for at least a few hours afterwards, they then forced a whole bag of saline solution into her and within less than an hour, she passed away as I was by her bedside.

I am convinced that my mother would have been alive today if I had the knowledge back then that I have today. I would have been able to help her before her high blood pressure deteriorated into hypertension and then into a stroke. But as painful as it was and still is, her death and this traumatic experience are what really spurred me on to find answers.

I am so grateful that I have now gained the understanding and knowledge through the incredible training and numerous courses I have taken with some incredible people, along with my own experiences to be able to help myself and others who want help. I still have a lot to learn, we all do, and we can never stop learning. Our health journey is about searching and discovering what works best for us. We are all different, we have been in different circumstances, have different diets and what may work for one person may not work for you, but there are some simple health basics we can all follow and benefit from that I will share soon.

I was not happy with the fact that my mother had been put on so many tablets as I was always against tablets and medication myself. I somehow knew with my limited knowledge back then that the tablets would not treat her condition.

After experiencing blood clots in my leg, I was placed on blood-thinning medications such as Warfarin and Heparin and told that I would have to take those for the rest of my life. But I would only take the medication when I was in hospital. After I came out of hospital and finished my course of medication, I never continued on them. I am not advocating that you do this.

If you decide to go the natural route, let your doctor know, he probably will not advocate it because his knowledge of nutritional healing may be limited, but go with your heart. You do not need permission to eat a natural, healing, nutritious diet.
Change your diet, and as you start to get better, then ask your doctor to slowly reduce your medication, monitoring you until he feels that you do not need them anymore. I am very happy I did not continue on medication after I left hospital, as recently a very good friend informed me that her father who lived in the UK had been on Warfarin for blood thinning for a few years and nearly died because the medication had damaged all of his organs. This was part of the side effects. He has sadly now passed away.

Besides when I was pregnant in 2004 when they had me injecting myself daily in the thigh with blood-thinning medication, I had not taken any penicillin or blood thinning medication in almost 30 years and have not had any need to since. As I get my blood circulating through natural foods such as garlic and cayenne pepper.

Doctors and hospitals do have their place. If I had an accident or an emergency such as a broken bone or did not know what was wrong, I would go to the hospital to be checked or for a diagnosis. If they decided to put me on medication, I would probably take it as long as I was under their care but work hard on improving my situation naturally to allow my body to heal.
Two weeks ago, on the 31st of August 2015, in the same week I should have released this book, I miraculously survived an

airplane crash in water, on a small aircraft. I escaped with minor injuries to my chin and teeth, the doctors and nurses in France were amazing in the way they took care of me, when I got back to the UK the dental doctor did an incredible job in pushing my lower teeth back into place. And I was certainly grateful for the painkillers. I also took the medication they gave me, although I knew they would make my body toxic, but once I completed the medication I made sure I detoxed my entire body. So hospitals certainly have their place. And I will be forever grateful in what they did for me.

But in the past in relation to my sickle cell, as soon as I came out of hospital, I would work hard on improving the problem naturally because I know that it's not the doctor or the hospital's responsibility to keep us well. The responsibility is all ours to make sure we do not suffer from nutritionally related illnesses; our responsibility is prevention through eating the correct life-giving foods rather than dead processed foods that can harm or even kill. Or at least cleansing the body occasionally to remove toxins that could cause issues down the line.

I also now know that medication drugs do not cure, they cannot; a cure comes only when you give the body what it needs to heal itself. When you give the body the correct life-giving fuel such as living whole nutrition and living water to help the body cleanse itself and function correctly, then the body has something to work with, so can therefore begin to heal itself naturally as it was designed to do.

If you do have to go to hospital, be sure to take your own healthy living nutritious foods and drinks or have someone take you some. The food and drinks in hospitals are the typical sloppy dead, processed, sugary and starchy foods that may have contributed to getting you there in the first place and will probably keep you there longer. If I was diagnosed with a nutritionally related condition, which most conditions are, I think I would be better off going to a naturopath or a nutritional doctor that is likely to know what to do without making the situation worse or making the body more toxic.

After becoming more responsible for my eating habits and starting to feel better, I began to look further into nutrition and the foods I was eating as the missing link to my complete healing. I cut out all junk foods and eventually all processed foods and to properly cleanse my body, I cut out all animal products and fish, especially farmed fish; this is genetically modified fish, grown outside of their natural environment, which we will mention more about later. This was after I discovered what was going into these foods, and I refused to contaminate my body with these chemicals, hormones and toxins that were contained in them and were contributing to the worsening of my condition. This gave my body a break and a chance to begin the cleansing and healing process.

I then cut out dairy and began to eat whole foods, super foods, raw foods (as in raw fruits and vegetables), living foods, nuts, seed, pulses, legumes, healthy vegan foods. (Some of the original diet for humans.) I began to see my health improve dramatically, starting with more energy and restored normal sleeping patterns, no daily aches or pains, constipation or infections.

Just great health and my blood count now normal to the amazement of my hospital consultant. My consultant who has now retired was even advising his other haematology patients of the importance of nutrition when he discovered this is what keeps me well. When you find a doctor that knows about nutrition and advises it, this is a real compassionate doctor. You know that they really care and want to help their patients. I am happy that more and more doctors are opening up to the facts of healing through nutrition.

After this change in my diet, the longest I spent out of hospital was 12 years, and in that time I did not even get a cold because I had built up my immune system by eating nutritious living foods, the type of foods that my body needed to nourish my cells and keep me healthy as well as supplementing my diet with natural plant-based minerals and vitamin supplements.

This is something I have to keep up daily. I have a daily protocol that keeps me well. It's a lifestyle to stay well. It's also a lifestyle to get sick. I once heard these sayings, "A man makes his own sick bed and lays in it." And, "The man that has no time for his health, will soon have time for nothing else."

I noticed at the beginning of my health journey that when I deliberately took good nutrients out of my diet as a test, I felt myself getting weak and tired, and when I put the nutrients back into my system, I felt completely well again. I did this because I had to prove to myself that it was what I was doing with the diet change that was keeping me well and healthy.

The same thing happens when I eat too many cooked foods and not enough raw vegetables; I feel sluggish, sleepy, my energy feels depleted, but when I eat a good amount of raw living whole foods, I get a burst of energy that lasts all day. If you give the body what it needs, the body will do what it's supposed to do — continue to heal itself naturally and stay in a good state of repair, balance and great health. Because I have built up my immune system and deeply cleanse my body regularly, I can now eat healthy cooked food without the tired, sluggish feeling.

I ended up in hospital with a sickle cell crisis after quite a few years of being in an over-stressful situation and losing my baby at eight months in the womb. I had suspected that I was going to get sick before it happened as I was stressed to the max. I had a lot of stress and tension, before, during and after my pregnancy, in having to deal with my mother's estate, a strained relationship and other stresses in my life and losing other family members, properties and absolutely everything.

But it did not surprise me when I got sick after being well for so long prior to this because I somehow instinctively knew that no matter how well you eat and take in good nutrition, plus learning through experience that if you do not get stress out of your body, it will deplete your immune system so you cannot fight infection and disease. We have heard that stress is a big killer; I believe that this can literally be true.

One thing I feel very important to share is that when I was pregnant, as well as having to inject myself with a poisonous substance, I had a couple of mercury or amalgam fillings removed, they are the same thing. I did not know how poisonous mercury fillings were at the time, and the dentist did not know either; otherwise, they may have advised against taking them out while pregnant.

My knowledge of mercury fillings today has taught me that mercury or amalgam fillings are the second most toxic substance on the planet next to plutonium. They are absolutely lethal and should not be used in people's mouths; I am shocked to discover that some dentists today still think it's OK to put or leave this second most toxic substance in people's mouths. There are holistic dentists that do not use them and some conventional dentists are aware and no longer use them.

When we were younger, they filled our mouths with them unnecessarily. I had suspected this when I got older, but I couldn't prove it. But it was proven when I went to the dentist after a fall that broke two top back teeth, in which I also had the remaining few amalgam filling removed and replaced; the dentist told me that some of the holes were so tiny that he did not understand why they were filled with mercury fillings in the first place. I have heard this same story from other people of my age group or older who had mercury fillings unnecessarily.

Well, I am bold to say that it's because they made more money on us, and I would not be surprised if the tiny holes were created in perfect young teeth just for profit, so it seems like the more mouths they filled with poison the more money they made. The dentist I went to in Spain after I had my fall, revealed to me that they get gifts and holidays as an incentive to use more drugs on customers. I had heard about this before but was shocked that the dentist was actually bold enough to admit this to me.

My recent research revealed that mercury also crosses the placenta, and when they were removed whilst pregnant, I had more toxic fumes released into my system and this is what I believe poisoned my baby. They couldn't find anything wrong with him during the post-mortem, but I'm sure if they had taken readings for mercury levels at the time, they would have been extremely high and would have found the cause.

So my advice is do not under any circumstances have mercury fillings removed when you're pregnant. If you have mercury fillings you should have them removed as soon as possible as they are slowly leaching into your body and poisoning you and may even be the cause of health problems you may be going through. People have had certain conditions reverse by having their mercury or amalgam filling removed and replaced with non-toxic fillings. Make sure you go to a holistic dentist that knows how to remove them safely without any toxic fumes being released back into your system, otherwise you could end up worse off.

If you are having dental problems, a good book I would recommend is "Cure Tooth Decay" by Ramiel Nagel. He gives very good insights on the truths of modern dentistry and how you can heal cavities naturally.

Now that I have taken the stress out of my body and continue to put the correct oxygen rich foods into my system along with simple daily and deeper periodic cleansing of my entire body, I can say that my blood count is normal. I noticed in a live blood analysis about four years ago that I had reversed at least 50% of the sickled cells in my blood and I'm working on reversing all of them completely, and I know this will happen very soon. In my most recent live blood analysis about a year ago I saw that about 90% of my cells were the normal oval shape and healthy looking, it's so exciting.

My healing protocol – This is my daily routine for staying well and healthy

I start in the morning with thoughts of having a great day. Then I go into my daily cleansing routine of oiling pulling for 20 minutes while in the shower, (more explanation on this further down), I brush my teeth with a natural tooth paste or my own homemade from extra virgin cold pressed coconut oil and bicarbonate of soda mixed into a paste. After this I drink one 8 oz. glass of living water and another glass containing my fizzy minerals and taking my supplement along with the fluids. After 10 minutes I have my lemon juice in warm water. 30 minutes later I usually have a green smoothie or juice, then I would have my home made non-dairy and non-soy yogurt alternative or a natural home-made granola with coconut or almond milk. An hour or 2 later, I would do my exercises including rebounding and facial exercises (more on this later) drinking plenty of water throughout the day and positive thoughts. Lunch and dinner would normally be healthy, and I would usually try to get to bed early, if possible between 10 and 11 after my shower and second set of facial exercises and gratitude prayer for the day. And that's my routine that keeps me healthy and out of hospital.

It may take a bit of work on your part, but you can find a health routine that works for you.
I never get sick, and I have a biological age of an 18-year-old, meaning my cardiovascular system is operating as that of an 18-year-old. The other bonus for eating living foods, detoxing and taking care of myself is that I do not have a problem with wrinkles and accelerated ageing.

But there was a period a few years ago where I was eating mainly cooked foods and noticed that I was beginning to age faster, I was then able to reverse this again by eating more living raw foods.

Ageing slowly was thought mainly to do with our genes, but recent studies show that ageing slowly amounts to only 10% responsible to our genes, so 90% must be due to nutrition, feeding your cells and lifestyle. I personally believe it's a bit more than 10%. I would also say raw living foods and cleansing the body of accumulated waste also contributes to a younger appearance as I have experienced, as well as other amazing benefits. Activated stabilised oxygen drops are also great for a more youthful skin, it's available to purchase in health food shops or online. We no longer have the same oxygen capacity in our lungs and environment that we had years ago due to the pollution of the earth, so it's very beneficial.

A friend who is an identical twin, has actually reduced 20 years off of his physical appearance and has lost over 15 kilos in excess weight since I told him about raw living foods and cleansing, he put this to practice and it was quite amazing seeing a recent photo of him standing next to his twin brother, it was more like father and son. This also proved to me that it is not all in the genes but to do with nutrition, oxygen, lifestyle and cleansing the body. It also tells me that you can change your genes by giving the body the correct nutrition and fuel.

Most people do not realise that the three secrets to ageing slowly and great health are eating raw living uncontaminated foods and water, periodic cleansing of all internal organs and oxygen therapy. There are also many other anti-ageing therapies and nutrients, I will share more with you later.

I am still mistaken by a lot people for being below 30 years young, although I am now 53 years young and always shock others when they discover my age.

compartments, components and characteristics in order to create the complete, perfect model the designer set out to create.

Before manufacturing the car, the designer also needs to decide what type of fuel the car will run on, whether the car will be run on petrol, diesel or electricity in order to build certain components into the car to facilitate this.

Once the car is complete, the manufacturer will include a handbook to instruct the driver on how the car works and runs. If the designer has designed the car to run on petrol and you decide to use diesel, the car will break down very quickly or not start at all.

When our body was designed, our designer had to factor in certain compartments, components and characteristics for the body to function correctly.

The body just like a car also needs to be taken care of and maintained correctly to run smoothly, it needs to be cleaned both in and out, a regular check up to see that every part is in good working order as well as requiring the correct foods (fuel) to run smoothly.

If our designer has designed our body to run on living whole oxygen rich electric foods full of living enzymes and nutrition that is needed for the smooth running of the entire body and you decide to use dead foods void of nutrition and living enzymes and full of toxic chemicals, the body will eventually break down, sooner or later because you are using the wrong fuel. So it may not be a matter of "if," but when will the body break down?

A CAR AND THE HUMAN BODY

To recap, our bodies like a car need the correct fuel (clean nutrition, clean water and clean oxygen to run smoothly).

A CAR NEEDS

- To be maintained to work correctly
- If your car needs petrol and you decide to put diesel into it, it will break down very quickly or not start
- A Clean Engine
- A Regular Service, which includes
- Oil change
- Tire check
- Checks to ensure the brakes, clutch and gas are in good working order
- To be regularly cleaned both in and out
- If the car has been taken care of, it will be given a good bill of health, an M.O.T.

THE HUMAN BODY NEEDS

- To be maintained to work correctly
- The correct fuel (living whole nutrition, fats, clean water and oxygen) to run smoothly. E.g.
- Living enzymes in raw living foods, good fats, mainly in foods such as avocado, coconut oil, hemp oil, nuts and seeds etc., vitamins, minerals, amino acids and nutrients to function correctly but most people are deficient and their bodies are breaking down due to the wrong type of fuel.

- Clean internal organs to ensure our organs are free to function properly.
- Regular check-ups, to see what is going on, both on the inside as well as the outside of our bodies to ensure everything is in good working order.
- To be cleaned both in and out.

Most of us clean our bodies once or twice a day, but how often do we clean our insides? Or maybe you did not realise this was possible or even necessary. This is so important and can even prevent and reverse chronic conditions. Even if you feel you cannot change your diet completely, do your best and include a daily and periodic cleanse of the entire body and this can prevent you from getting a host of health problems. Detoxing is now very popular compared to before, but most people because of the foods they are consuming need a deep periodic cleanse of all internal organs.

The human body was designed to cleanse itself internally through certain organs such as the colon, liver, kidneys and lymphatic systems and using the correct living foods and herbs. But an acidic, inflamed, toxic environment in the body caused by dead processed foods, too much alcohol, prescription and recreational drugs, causes the body to become polluted, and so needs help in cleansing the accumulated waste on a regular basis to avoid disease of the body.

Our body and organs know what to do; we just need to help them by giving them the correct fuel and building blocks to do the work. The human body needs to be cleansed internally of the accumulated waste to get a cleaner system and to promote proper blood and oxygen circulation that will bring healing. When the blood is clean, oxygenated and circulating well, it will send fresh blood to promote healing in the areas of the body that is not doing so well.

Nourish the cells with proper nutrition to build the organs back up and get the organs to function correctly, and this will balance the whole body to heal itself of almost anything naturally.

(We will talk more in detail about internal body cleansing soon)

The Problem

Again, the problem is too much build-up of accumulated waste in the body, as a result of what we consume and ingest daily. Accumulation in the form of human waste, excess mucus, parasites, heavy metals, radiation and toxic waste creates an acidic, inflamed environment in our body. It wreaks havoc on our organs and immune system and causes a lack of proper blood circulation resulting in stagnant, thick, dirty sticky blood and the perfect breeding ground for disease.

Inflammation is like brushing an open sore, and this is best healed with plant-based nutrition; it cannot be thoroughly healed with anti-inflammatory tablets, which is only temporary and mask the symptoms, eventually causing other problems. In the process of blood stagnation, our organs are also strained as a result of lack of circulating blood. Also a deficiency of essential vitamins, minerals and nutrients that the body needs to function and heal itself are missing as a result of taking in the wrong fuel, creating major problems with our health.

The process as a result of eating lifeless acidic foods

| Accumulation of human waste, excess mucus, parasites, toxins, heavy metals and radiation | | Lack of proper blood circulation, causing thick, dirty and stagnant blood | | Deficiency of essential vitamins, minerals, amino acids and nutrients |

What happens if not addressed and you continue on this path?

| The body goes into toxic overload and the cells begin to get sick | | The organs begin to deteriorate, do not function correctly and may eventually break down | | You begin to get minor complaints like lack of energy, headache and constipation, until it leads to a chronic condition |

The Solution

The solution is to **Cleanse** the blood, colon, liver, kidneys, gallbladder, lymphatic system and all vital organs of the body of accumulated waste that have been in the body for decades, increasing in toxicity and acidity daily.

Cleaning backed-up human waste from the bowels, parasites from our body, excess mucus from the cells, organs and entire body, plaque from the arteries and an arm's list of toxins as well as heavy metals and radiation, will allow good circulation of blood to flow again. The body will be **Regulated** and in balance so as to begin the rejuvenation process and heal itself naturally as it was designed to do.

Nourish the cells by replacing essential missing vitamins, minerals, amino acids and nutrients to build the immune system, heal and restore the organs of the body to function normally and promote healing of the entire body, mind and skin.

Cleanse the body of accumulated human waste, excess mucus, parasites, toxins and radiation	➡	Regulate the organs to start functioning correctly to begin the healing and rejuvenation	➡	Nourish the body by replacing the missing essential vitamins, minerals amino acids and nutrients

Just as we take good care of our cars, we also need to take even better care of our health and body, but, unfortunately, some take better care of their cars and physical appearance more than their health because they cannot see what is going on inside and assume everything is OK. Our health is often neglected because we may be feeling relatively well on the outside, so we assume all is well. We often dismiss minor aches, pains and niggles as nothing, but this is your body speaking to you and telling you there is something going wrong.

The human body is a very strong but complex machine, it may not break down as quickly as a car, but every time we take the wrong fuel (foods) into our system, unless you are doing regular cleanses, it leaves a mark in the body. This then accumulates until it manifests into a condition.

This is sadly happening far too often, and people are unaware that most of this can not only be prevented but also reversed by a change of diet and engaging in periodic cleansing, that can act as a prevention. Unfortunately, I have seen this far too often, even with people who I knew, who are no longer here to tell their story.

Taking steps to make sure that we do not become part of the statistics is the first thing to do. Many people suffering from minor or chronic conditions are put on drugs for the rest of their lives, and some die unexpectedly and prematurely and it's getting worse, but this does not have to be your fate.

You can begin to see great results if you do not take your health for granted and start taking the steps towards prevention and great health. The ever increasing statistics are too high to assume it will not happen to us, especially if you are unaware of what's really in your food and products.

If I were to ask you how important your health is to you, you would probably say very important.

Answer these four questions to see how important your health really is to you.

- How often do you go for a check up to see what is going on inside your body?
- How much do you invest in your health on a monthly or yearly basis?
- How often do you do an internal cleanse of your organs or a detox?
- How much health research do you do for yourself?

Considering that chronic conditions are increasing drastically each year, we would all benefit from doing these things, unless you are already active in this area.

It is not too expensive to do yearly tests through a nutritional doctor or naturopath to make sure all is well on the inside.

"Our Health is our most important asset. Without it we can do nothing."

If you prioritise your health and take good care of your body, the same way you take care of your car, it will have its M.O.T, an automatic bill of excellent health. There will be no need for you to get sick and you can be confident of this as long as you make staying healthy part of your lifestyle.

Your body and organs will be balanced and in the correct working order, rejuvenating your whole body daily as it gets the correct fuel, you will have good circulation going, your cells and body will be clean, nourished and oxygenated, your immune system will be strengthened to be able to fight off anything that comes along, and you will have an added bonus of ageing much slower or even reverse ageing, which is a normal result of eating clean, living foods.

So to start, the main thing is to focus on the cause of the condition rather than the symptom, if your condition is being caused by something, does it not make sense to find out what is causing it, so you can stop or avoid this?

As mentioned before, in the medical world, symptoms are treated with drugs that cannot cure or treat the cause.

So when you seek treatment for your condition, seek the health pathway that will add to your life and not subtract from it.

Disease is the body's way of adapting to an unnatural environment, so symptoms occur to protect your body. A symptom is your body speaking to you and telling you there is something wrong.

Symptoms are just given many different names, but it's all mainly the same causes of accumulation in the body, lack of blood circulation and deficiency of the essential fuel the body needs for maintenance.

There is a great fear of the dreaded and mysterious Cancer and it's on the increase as we all know and effecting many people. My heart goes out to all that have lost their battle against it. Although in medicine it still remains a mystery and seen as a condition that there is no cure for.   But I learnt from one of my mentors, that Cancer is a symptom of an accumulation of localised toxins in varies parts of the body.

So in other words, lung cancer equals localised toxins in the lung, breast and prostate cancer equals localised toxins in the breast and prostate. Leukaemia (blood cancer) equals localised toxins in the blood. This made so much more sense to me and is possibly the reason why some people are healing themselves of cancer by changing to a vegan diet that detoxes and cleanses the body. I know people who have cured themselves from cancer using this method.

CHAPTER 2

What price are you paying for stress?

We all have a level of stress if we live on planet earth, but being over-stressed is where the danger comes in, this can be a killer and can cause:

- Errors
- Risk of sickness
- Conflict
- Low morale
- Days off sick
- Poor decisions/indecision
- Risk of heart attack
- Migraines
- Tiredness
- Anger
- Feeling hopeless
- Accidents

It is now well known that stressful conditions suppress the immune response. Whether physical or psychological, stress stimulates the body's fight-or-flight response. The brain's emotional centres send a message to the hypothalamus, which signals the pituitary gland.

Directives are sent from the pituitary gland to the body to prepare for an attack to (fight or flee). The heart rate speeds up at this moment; the fats, cholesterol and sugar in the blood stream increase, the stomach secretes more acid, which leaves a feeling of fear.

Stress is also associated with changes in thyroid hormones, our body can also be stressed by the growth hormones found in the foods we eat, both of which suppress the immune function. The body's vitamins and trace elements such as A, B complex, C and Zinc are decreased further by stress so cannot be utilised appropriately.

This results in further deficiencies that can impair immune function and cause other problems in the body. Some physical stresses include fear, accidents, trauma, extreme cold or body chills, exercising to exhaustion, relational, loss, pain or very loud noise, as well as stress on the body and cells from eating dead foods. Stress and worry as most of us know, also cause accelerated ageing and greying of the hair.

Stress can be reduced with deep slow breathing from the lower abdomen, or you can join a local group that teaches stress reduction techniques to alleviate the over-stressed condition of your body.

The correct way of breathing is extremely important to your good health in keeping the body oxygenated, which helps with your blood circulation and oxygen levels, breathing correctly relaxes the muscles and reduces stress and tension in the body. The correct breathing can also help the body to detoxify.

We should instinctively know the correct way of breathing, but due to stress, our breathing can be very shallow from the chest without being aware, rather than slow deep breathing from the abdomen, which is the correct way of breathing. We seem to lose the art of breathing as we get older, watch a baby breathing, they instinctively know to breath from the abdomen and not the chest. Be aware to breathe slowly and deeply from the lower abdomen rather than shallow breathing from the chest.

When you breathe correctly, your stomach should expand on inhaling and contract on exhaling. Just like blowing air into a balloon, it expands and then contracts when the air is released. You can practice this to help you get back into the correct way of breathing.

What price are you paying for your stress? What do you need to change? Like myself, you may not even be aware that you are over-stressed until I collapsed from exhaustion and burn out. Try the Stress Test to see if you are in danger of burning out.

THE STRESS TEST

If you are suffering from stress, you may notice some of the following signs and symptoms. Stress is seen as a major contributing factor in many conditions. Stress comes in many forms, we can also have stress in our body from toxins around us as well as those we ingest.

- Feeling sweaty or having shivers
- Pounding heart or palpitations
- Needing to go to the toilet frequently
- Feeling sick in the stomach or (butterflies)
- Dry mouth
- Exhaustion
- Unusual aches and pains
- Drinking and smoking more
- Headaches
- Irritable
- Feeling of pointlessness
- Loss of appetite for food, fun and sex
- Loss of interest in others
- Loss of memory
- Loss of interest in personal appearance

- Forgetfulness
- Tearfulness
- Lack of energy
- Difficulty sleeping
- Disturbed sleep

Note: Some of these symptoms can also be a symptom of other conditions of the body.

CHAPTER 3

Why is this epidemic of sickness raging?

Artificial processed foods or man-made foods manufactured to taste good but are extremely addictive and, in my opinion, the new drug addiction that have become the norm.
Fuelled by advertising campaigns, people are duped into believing that these dead foods are somehow good for them.

These foods also contain ingredients and substances that are pure chemicals and cause cravings, there is very little difference between addictions, whether it's drugs, alcohol, cigarettes or food addictions; the more you eat these substances, the more you become addicted, and the more accumulation builds up, and the more susceptible you are for your cells and body to deteriorate.
It is this addiction that makes it very difficult for people to stop eating foods they may know are bad for them.

We are eating more man-made foods that the body finds difficult to digest, and in some cases does not know what to do with or cannot eliminate completely, they are not real food, just manufactured food-like substances that tastes like food and just to increase sales; you are left with undigested waste and toxins in your system rotting for years. This contributes to body odour, bad breath and smelly stool, this waste becomes like tar and is often very difficult to remove.
Such waste can often only be removed using bitter herbs or minerals such as magnesium oxide for deep cleansing of the colon.

Nutritional Deficiency of our food and body

As mentioned before, nutritional deficiency is one of the main reasons the problem of sickness is increasing. Below, I have explained the six reasons why we are not getting all the nutrition from our foods and why we may also need Nutritional Supplements to combat nutritional deficiency.

1. Green Harvesting

Fruits and Vegetables picked when still green and unripe.
Example, tomatoes picked when green and pumped full of gas to produce the bright red colour. This gives it shelf life, but very little if any nutritional value. Have you noticed that when you buy non organic fruits and vegetables nowadays, they can keep for a very long time before rotting? This is great for the prolonged shelf life of the food and the pockets of the suppliers, but not for your body because the little nutrition that may be in the food is insufficient for the body to work with.

2. Foods cooked at a very high temperature

The nutrition and enzymes in our foods are further killed off when cooked beyond 109°F (42°C). This changes the chemical structure of the food, which causes toxins to accumulate and stresses our body. We are better off eating our vegetables in its most raw natural state as much as possible. Or steaming them for just two minutes should be enough not to destroy all the enzymes completely, but, of course, raw is always best, especially when it comes to the purpose of cleansing foods for cleansing the body.

When we cook, the nutrients in the food will begin to evaporate at about 95 degrees, and become carcinogenic (Cancer causing) at about 102 degrees. By 115 degrees, the nutrients begin to mutate, become deformed and degenerated, losing all their nutrients. The body no longer recognises it as food, so treats it as a toxin. This is why so many people are nutritionally deficient. Because the body doesn't recognise the substance as food, people still continue to eat when they are full, not because they are still hungry, but because their body needs the nutrients that it did not get from the overcooked foods they have just eaten. So it is important to get a good proportion of raw food daily in your diet.

Raw fruits, vegetables, chlorophyll found in green vegetables such as spinach, kale and certain grasses such as wheatgrass and barley grass, sprouted seeds and sprouted beans such as alfalfa, chickpeas and mung beans etc. are living foods (when sprouted). Sprouting means soaking them in water, changing the water daily for a few days until the beans or seeds begin to sprout white or green shoots. These foods contain life-giving enzymes that bring energy, life and healing to the body and, in fact, sprouts are still growing as you are eating them; they taste great in salads too. Just a word on the cruciferous family of vegetables such as broccoli, cauliflower, cabbage, Brussels sprouts and kale. If you have an impaired digestive system, which most people do nowadays, it may be difficult for you to digest them raw, so you can either take digestive enzymes when eating these foods raw or make sure you boil them lightly before eating until you heal your digestive system.

Live foods = health and a long healthy life for the body. Dead foods = disease and premature death for the body. "Life creates life."

3. Reduced Nutrient Contents Because of soil depletion and chemical sprays

The Nutritional content in our fruits and vegetables has dramatically reduced compared to 60 years ago as a result of soil depletion and chemical sprays on our food. A study in the Sunday Times in the year 2000 reported the reduced nutrient contents and gave alarming statistics on this. For example, it showed that there is 75% less calcium in broccoli compared to 60 years ago. Below are more examples of nutritional depletion in our foods:

- 75% Less magnesium in carrots
- 67% Less iron in oranges
- 60% Less iron in spinach
- 55% Less calcium in strawberries
- 45% Less magnesium in melons

Chemicals are not only sprayed on the food, but they are now added to the roots of the food so every part of that food will contain chemicals. So sacrifice and buy organic or grow your own if you can, that's even better, and you will limit the amount of toxins you take into your system.

4. Impaired Villi

Very often through poor eating habits, smoking and drinking, the Villi, in the lower intestines, responsible for taking up the nutrients from the food into the blood, becomes impaired, it gets covered in mucus so it cannot work effectively. Therefore, it cannot absorb the nutrition from the foods we are eating.

So, with even the most purest and organic foods and supplements, if we are not absorbing the nutrients into the blood or cannot digest our food, we will benefit very little from the food. This is why internal body cleansing is so important to remove all blockages, and to help food digest quicker, chew your food till its liquid in the mouth because digestion begins in the mouth, and this will help your digestive system to digest the food properly and quicker.

5. Artificial foods.
We are not eating real foods; if you eat processed foods, they are not real foods, you are eating acidic, chemical products that have

been artificially manufactured to look like food and taste like food, containing additives and toxins, but they are not food, they do not feed you, they only cause accumulation and an acidic environment in the body, oxidative stress and free radical damage to cells and entire body that leads to disease of the body.

6. Hybrid and GMO foods

I have known for some time that certain seedless foods are hybrid foods because everything needs a seed to reproduce itself. Anything without a seed has been produced by the manipulation of man and cannot grow unaided, so we become dependent on man for our foods rather than Mother Nature.

I have recently been learning that some of our foods such as wheat, carrots, except for wild black carrot and many other foods did not originally grow naturally. I have learnt that they came about by cross-breeding two different types of vegetables to get these certain species of foods. As man cannot create natural nutrition, it would be suspected that these foods do not have any nutritional value or very little and may contain toxins and additives. You may find some other hybrid foods as you research.

I am still researching this, but hybrid foods are probably also the reason so many people have wheat and other food allergies because the foods have been crossbred or tampered with. This also goes for genetically modified foods (GMO) which I have learnt are causing a host of health problems and birth defects whilst poisoning the body. I urge you to do your research on this so you can come up with your own conclusion, and as I mentioned before, if we avoid these substances and don't spend money on them, they will stop manufacturing them. Also, a lot of GMOs are not labelled, especially in the USA, this is why it's important to find your local organic farmer and support them. More on GMO further down.

Below is a list of some natural electric non-hybrid foods as originally found in nature and the correct fuel created by Mother Nature that the body needs to sustain itself.

These foods were identified by Dr Sebi of the Usha Research Institute who identified that we are electric beings and, therefore, require electric foods to function correctly.

Non-Hybrid Alkaline Foods

RECOMMENDED FOODS ALKALINE FOODS

Amaranth greens – same as Callaloo, a variety of Spinach
Avocado
Asparagus
Bell Peppers
Burro Banana
Chayote (Mexican Squash)
Cucumber
Dandelion greens
Garbanzo beans (chickpeas) optional
Izote – cactus flower/ cactus leaf grows naturally in California
Jicama
Kale
Lettuce (all, except Iceberg)
Mushrooms (all, except Shitake)
Mustard greens
Nopales – Mexican Cactus
Okra
Olives
Onions
Poke salad -greens
Sea Vegetables (wakame/dulse/arame/hijiki/nori)
Squash
Spinach (use sparingly)
String beans

Tomato – cherry and plum only
Tomatillo
Turnip greens
Zucchini (courgettes)

RECOMMENDED FOODS

FRUITS - no canned or seedless fruits

Apples
Bananas – the smallest one or the Burro/mid-size (original banana)
Berries – all varieties. Elderberries in any form – no cranberries
Cantaloupe
Cherries
Currants
Dates
Figs
Grapes -seeded
Limes (key limes preferred with seeds)
Mango
Melons -seeded
Orange (Seville or sour preferred, difficult to find)
Papayas
Peaches
Pears
Plums
Prunes
Raisins -seeded
Soft Jelly Coconuts
Sour sops –Latin or West Indian markets)
Sugar apples (cherimoya)

ALL NATURAL HERBAL TEAS
Alvaca
Anise
Chamomile
Cloves
Fennel
Ginger
Lemon grass
Red Raspberry
Sea Moss Tea

SPICES & SEASONINGS

Mild Flavours
Basil
Bay leaf
Cilantro
Dill
Marjoram
Oregano
Sweet Basil
Tarragon
Thyme

Pungent & Spicy Flavours
Achiote
Cayenne
Cumin
Coriander
Onion Powder
Sage

Salty Flavours
Pure Sea Salt
Powdered Granulated Seaweed

(Kelp/Dulce/Nori – has "sea taste")

Sweet Flavours
100% Pure Maple Syrup – Grade B recommended
Maple "Sugar" (from dried maple syrup)
Date "Sugar" (from dried dates)
100% Pure Agave Syrup – (from cactus)

NUTS & SEEDS - (includes Nut & Seed Butters)
Raw Almonds and Almond butter
Raw Sesame Seeds
Raw Sesame "Tahini" Butter
Walnuts
Hazelnuts

Dr Sebi says that he cannot be sure of any foods outside of this list.

Conclusion: Our body needs support with taking in the correct nutrients.

We are not getting the correct amount of nutrients or fuel that our body needs to:

- Function correctly
- Produce the correct amount of oxygen
- Fight free radicals damage
- Cleanse itself
- Heal itself
- Build a strong immune system
- Fight disease
- Keep our energy levels high
- Give us rejuvenation and longevity

Thanks to man's interferences, we have much against us. And as you have seen, we are not getting all of the nutrition that we need even from some of the natural living plant-based foods that we expect to get it from.

Although we are no longer getting the full nutrient content in our fruits and vegetables, we can reduce further loss by not boiling our vegetables to death, as most of the nutrients are lost in the water that is thrown away.

Steaming our vegetables slightly is far better. They will stay crunchy, which is much healthier than soft, soggy veggies. Even better is eating the vegetables raw or grated into salads, as you will get more of the living enzymes and nutrients that the body needs to work with in keeping you disease free.

It's more beneficial if you can buy organic or unsprayed, but if you can't afford to, then make sure you wash your fruits and vegetables with lemon juice or apple cider vinegar, this is very good for removing some of the chemicals and toxins from fruits and vegetables, this also reduces the amount of chemicals and toxins you take into your body.

Even better, if you have the space and a bit of time, grow your own. It's much healthier and cheaper and you know what you're eating. You will be surprised what you can grow on your window ledge or in your kitchen if you don't have a garden.

Nutritional Supplements

If you're eating non-organic food, or not growing your own food, then you will definitely benefit from nutritional supplements. As you have seen from the information above, we are not getting our full spectrum of vitamins, minerals and nutrients from our foods for various reasons, so it is important to supplement our diets to make sure we are getting enough nutrients for our body to work with. I would also say that because of soil depletion and chemicals in the air we breathe, everybody would benefit from taking nutritional supplements.

Unless you live on a pristine mountain somewhere in the world that has been virtually untouched by man, and because we live in a mostly toxic environment, I think we all need some sort of supplementation regularly or occasionally, not necessarily in the form of a capsule, but you can also supplement with super foods such as Moringa, Spirulina, Barley grass, or wheatgrass juice, etc. I don't believe that anything is 100% organic anymore because of the amount of toxins being released into our environment every day, but a certain percentage of natural organic is better than non-organic.

It is important when you buy nutritional supplements to make sure that they are plant-based from a food source and not man-made synthetic or metallic supplements. There are many nutritional supplements on the market, and many of them are synthetic supplements that can damage your body and only make your condition worse. They also are not effective.

Synthetic and metallic supplements do not assimilate into your system and simply come out in your urine, so you end up having expensive urine and not much benefit from the supplement you're taking. Synthetic supplement can even give off toxins in the body. They can also make cancers worse. Plant-based supplements with vegetable capsules are more easily absorbed into your system.

The market is flooded with supplements, but a good way of making sure you buy good quality nutritional supplements is to buy them from a specialist company that has a quality control and quality assurance department. You can also ask the company if they have a certificate of analysis based on third party analysis.

If you do buy them from a shop, make sure it's a proper organic health food shop rather than a chemist and other high street shops that sell synthetic supplements. If in doubt, read the label and search for the ingredients on the Internet to see what it contains. For the highest quality supplement, you also need to make sure that they are wild crafted.

This means that the ingredients are cultivated naturally from the wild because when the herbs are organically grown, they may not contain pesticides or chemicals, but they are often watered with ordinary tap water, which contains chlorine, fluoride, heavy metals, drug residue and other chemicals. This also goes for the food. But again, a percentage of organic is better than non-organic that may contain the whole array of toxins.

Also, before you start taking supplements, make sure you cleanse your entire system starting with your colon so that your body can absorb it. Vitamins are useless if your organs are clogged up. You will not get the full benefits from them. Also, make sure you take vitamins and minerals together as vitamins are virtually useless without the minerals, although minerals can be assimilated without vitamins, but it's more beneficial to take them both.

It is also a good idea and great health benefit to include chlorophyll as mentioned before from super foods, from the dark green leafy vegetables and foods such as kale, spinach, parsley, coriander and Moringa etc.

I personally think that Moringa that combats malnutrition, is needed for western malnutrition, even more so as we have a big problem with the increase of so many chronic conditions and people dying prematurely in our so-called developed countries. Chlorophyll is also great for the acid/alkaline balance.

You may have heard about alkalising the body, but this will cause problems if you attempt to alkalise the whole body, because parts of the body are alkaline while other parts are acid. For example, the stomach is acid and so is the skin, the mouth and other parts of the body are alkaline, so it may not be a good idea to try to make the whole body alkaline by taking too many alkaline products, you can throw the natural state of your body's Ph. out of balance. Taking these products may be beneficial if you are eating mainly acid foods, but eating a balanced organic plant-based diet should keep the correct alkaline/acid balance whilst eating processed food will make your body acidic.

Because we need to be more on the alkaline side, our Ph. should be at least 7 or slightly above, which is on the alkaline side. If your Ph. is lower than 7.0, you cannot absorb certain minerals and nutrients. For couples who want to conceive, you will find this difficult if you do not have enough amounts of certain minerals such as iron and manganese, and you can only absorb these minerals if your Ph. is at least 6.0 or above.

An acidic body also known as acidosis, is normally a pre-curser to disease.
But the moment you get rid of the toxic overload and the acid and replace it with alkaline foods, the body gets the correct acid/alkaline balance; that is more on the alkaline side, the body becomes oxygen-rich and begins to heal itself, your body at that moment will just do what it's designed to do and that is to create the perfect health and bring your body into balance. When you support it through cleansing and giving it the correct nutritious foods, it will put your body in the perfect condition to heal itself and create the perfect health and vitality for you.

Essential Nutrition for a healthy body

Nutrition is the elements in food that promote good health. There are over 40 essential nutrients to life that the body needs every day for optimum health including:

Vitamins

Minerals

Amino acids

Trace elements

Fatty acids

Fibre

You can get this all from a good balanced plant-based diet and supplementation.

As mentioned before, you can absorb minerals without vitamins but you cannot absorb vitamins without minerals, but at the same time, everybody is mineral deficient because of soil depletion; as mentioned before, the soil is no longer nutrient rich. You can make sure your body gets all the minerals it needs by taking a good natural mineral supplement from a good source of minerals from the sea, a liquid mineral or a tablet form. Make sure its natural and has no added binders, fillers or anything else.

The body also needs:

Fresh Air

Sunshine

Exercise

Relaxation

Oxygenating

Alkalisation/acid balance

Antioxidants

Cleansing/Detox the body

Cleansing/ Detox the mind from negative thoughts

Adequate Sleep

Healthy Relationships

Positive thoughts

De-stressing

Clean oxygenated living structured water

Water The Great Mystery

You may have heard that the human body is made up of up to 90% water, but the truth about water in my opinion has been greatly underestimated and the knowledge hidden. Hydration from water is needed for many functions of the body. Dehydration can cause many problems in the body and add to disease.

Water as found in nature and an unpolluted environment is a living, energised structured substance or life in liquid form. It is structured, meaning it is allowed to move freely around the rocks, down waterfalls, settled in a vortex system and is absolutely perfect. When water is polluted with toxins, chlorine, fluoride, drug residue and other chemicals, bottled and put into pipes with sharp curves and angles, the water loses its life-force and becomes dead water, without any life-force and drastically reduced benefits to the human body.

Water is the most common, yet the most important substance on earth. Every living thing needs water to survive. Water is used in many ways in different industries. Water is a cleanser, a healer, a nourisher and loaded with natural energy, vitamins and minerals.

Drinking energised and structured water will immediately replenish and separate cells that are stuck together due to the loss of their electrical charge, so much so, that the change can be immediately observed under a microscope. Something I have actually experienced myself in looking at my cells under a microscope before and after drinking living structured water. My cells were more separated and free after drinking living water. Structured energised water will allow the cells to carry oxygen again, as well as clean the cells and organs.

Some of the benefits of living structured water are immediate hydration into the cells, boosting the immune system, better absorption of nutrients, eliminates toxins, improves oxygen to the bloodstream and better blood circulation, activates enzymes and enhances muscle tone, weight loss, fewer headaches, longevity, balance Ph. levels with a Ph. of about 7.5, which is on the alkaline side, most other waters that come out of taps and bottles are acidic.

Structured energised water also sustains and regains human, animal and plant health and tastes much better and is much softer and carries with it only those vitamins and minerals that are good for life. Anything else in the body, such as heavy metals, toxins, etc. while taking structured water is flushed out of your elimination channels.

When you look at both structured energised water and non-structured water, they may both look the same in clarity, but after conducting a test, making ice cubes with both types of water, the ice made from the structured energised water was much clearer in appearance whilst the ice from the unstructured water was very cloudy looking.

Another test I did was to give two bowls of water to my brother's cat, one with ordinary tap water and the other filled with living water from a living water jug that I use and, of course, Bella the cat after sniffing both waters went straight for the living water. Animals know what is good and what is not.

The most remarkable thing I discovered is that water has memory. Water can pick up information and remembers it over time. Research has shown that as it flows along, it picks up different information along the way and remembers when it passes that area again.

Dr Masaru Emoto conducted various experiments on water, and what he found was nothing short of remarkable. In one experiment, he took three glass jars and placed some rice in each jar, covering them with water, and over a period of three months, he said thank you to one jar, you're an idiot to the second jar and completely ignored the third jar. After a month, the rice that he thanked began to ferment, giving off a strong pleasant aroma, the rice in the second jar turned black, and the rice that was ignored began to rot.

In another experiment, he exposed music, spoken words, typed words, pictures and videos of water. After he froze and crystallised each one, the water's response was amazing.

The words, love, thank you and appreciation, gratitude, peace, happiness, truth and music such as amazing grace and Beethoven's Pastorale and water exposed to a child, formed beautiful majestic crystals. Crystallised water taken from a lake after a prayer offering also showed beautiful majestic crystals.

But when words like, "you make me sick, I will kill you," Adolf Hitler, Demon, water exposed to anger and heavy metal music, the crystals formed very dark and sharp-edged shapes.

Since discovering this, I have made it a habit of thanking my drinking water and bath and shower water.

(Source :) and for more information on energised structured water, watch "water the great mystery" online, or you can buy the DVD. It's absolutely fascinating, and you will never see water in the same way again.

You can also see some of Dr Emoto's experiments on Internet.

Man-made foods –Genetically Modified Organisms

In 2009, the American Academy of Environmental Medicine (AAEM) stated that, "Several animal studies indicate serious health risks associated with genetically modified (GM) food," including infertility, immune problems, accelerated ageing, faulty insulin regulation, and changes in major organs and the gastrointestinal system. The AAEM has asked physicians to advise all patients to avoid GM foods.

Starting in 1996, Americans have been eating genetically modified (GM) ingredients in most processed foods. Why isn't the FDA protecting us?

In 1992, the Food and Drug Administration claimed they had no information showing that GM foods were substantially different from conventionally grown foods. Therefore, they are safe to eat, and absolutely no safety studies were required. But internal memos made public by a lawsuit reveal that their position was staged by political appointees who were under orders from the White House to promote GMOs. In addition, the FDA official in charge of creating this policy was Michael Taylor, the former attorney for Monsanto, the
largest biotech company, and later their vice president.

In reality, FDA scientists had repeatedly warned that GM foods can create unpredictable, hard-to-detect side effects, including allergies, toxins, new diseases, and nutritional problems. They urged long-term safety studies but were ignored.

Today, the same biotech companies who have been found guilty of hiding toxic effects of their chemical products are in charge of determining whether their GM foods are safe. Industry-funded GMO safety studies are too superficial to find most of the potential dangers, and their voluntary consultations with the FDA are widely criticised as a meaningless façade.

GM plants, such as soybean, corn, cottonseed, and canola, have had foreign genes forced into their DNA. The inserted genes come from species, such as bacteria and viruses, which have never been in the human food supply.

Genetic engineering transfers genes across natural species barriers. It uses imprecise laboratory techniques that bear no resemblance to natural breeding and is based on outdated concepts of how genes and cells work. Gene insertion is done either by shooting genes from a "gene gun" into a plate of cells or by using bacteria to invade the cell with foreign DNA. The altered cell is then cloned into a plant.

Widespread, unpredictable changes

The genetic engineering process creates massive collateral damage, causing mutations in hundreds or thousands of locations throughout the plant's DNA. Natural genes can be deleted or permanently turned on or off, and hundreds may change their behavior. Even the inserted gene can be damaged or rearranged, and may create proteins that can trigger allergies or promote disease.

GM foods on the market

There are eight GM food crops. The five major varieties — soy, corn, canola, cotton, and sugar beets — have bacterial genes inserted, which allow the plants to survive an otherwise deadly dose of weed killer. Farmers use considerably more herbicides on these GM crops, and so the food has higher herbicide residues. About 68% of GM crops are herbicide tolerant.

The second GM trait is a built-in pesticide, found in GM corn and cotton. A gene from the soil bacterium called Bt (for Bacillus thuringiensis) is inserted into the plant's DNA, where it secretes the insect-killing Bt-toxin in every cell. About 19% of GM crops produce their own pesticide. Another 13% produce a pesticide and are herbicide tolerant.

There is also Hawaiian papaya and a small amount of zucchini and yellow crookneck squash, which are engineered to resist a plant virus.

Growing evidence of harm from GMOs
GM soy and allergic reactions

- Soy allergies skyrocketed by 50% in the UK, soon after GM soy was introduced.
- A skin prick allergy test shows that some people react to GM soy, but not to wild natural soy.
- Cooked GM soy contains as much as seven times the amount of a known soy allergen.
- GM soy also contains a new, unexpected allergen, not found in wild natural soy.

Bt corn and cotton linked to allergies

The biotech industry claims that Bt-toxin is harmless to humans and mammals because the natural bacteria version has been used as a spray by farmers for years. In reality, hundreds of people exposed to Bt spray had allergic-type symptoms, and mice fed Bt had powerful immune responses and damaged intestines. Moreover, the Bt in GM crops is designed to be more toxic than the natural spray and is thousands of times more concentrated.

Farm workers throughout India are getting the same allergic reactions from handling Bt cotton as those who reacted to Bt spray. Mice and rats fed Bt corn also showed immune responses.

GMOs fail allergy tests

No tests can guarantee that a GMO will not cause allergies. Although the World Health Organisation recommends a screening protocol, the GM soy, corn, and papaya in our food supply fail

Functioning GM genes remain inside you

Unlike safety evaluations for drugs, there are no human clinical trials of GM foods. The only published human feeding experiment revealed that the genetic material inserted into GM soy transfers into bacteria living inside our intestines and continues to function. This means that long after we stop eating GM foods, we may still have their GM proteins produced continuously inside us.

- If the antibiotic gene inserted into most GM crops were to transfer, it could create super diseases, resistant to antibiotics.
- If the gene that creates Bt-toxin in GM corn were to transfer, it might turn our intestinal bacteria into living pesticide factories.
- Animal studies show that DNA in food can travel into organs throughout the body, even into the fetus.

GM food supplement caused deadly epidemic

In the 1980s, a contaminated brand of a food supplement called L-tryptophan killed about 100 Americans and caused sickness and disability in another 5,000-10,000 people. The source of contaminants was almost certainly the genetic engineering process used in its production. The disease took years to find and was almost overlooked. It was only identified because the symptoms were unique, acute, and fast-acting. If all three characteristics were not in place, the deadly GM supplement might never have been identified or removed.

If GM foods on the market are causing common diseases or if their effects appear only after long-term exposure, we may not be able to identify the source of the problem for decades if at all. There is no monitoring of GMO-related illnesses and no long-term animal studies. Heavily invested biotech corporations are gambling with the health of our nation for their profit.

Help end the genetic engineering of our food supply
When the tipping point of consumer concern about GMOs was achieved in Europe in 1999, within a single week virtually all major food manufacturers committed to remove GM ingredients. The Campaign for Healthier Eating in America is designed to reach a similar tipping point in the US soon.

Our growing network of manufacturers, retailers, healthcare practitioners, organisations, and the media, is informing consumers of the health risks of GMOs and helping them select healthier non-GMO alternatives with our Non-GMO Shopping Guides.

Start buying non-GMO today. Help stop the genetic engineering of our food supply. (Source: Institute for responsible technology)

CHAPTER 4

4 Common diets, which is best for you?

There are four common diets today that people eat.

1. Raw food diet
2. Vegan diet
3. Vegetarian diet
4. Animal-based Meat / fish diet

Raw Vegan Diet

The raw food diet is by far the best diet for cleansing the body and nutrition. It also keeps the body charged up with an abundance of energy when you eat enough of it. This way of eating has been known to reverse many chronic conditions. I believe it was the diet and correct fuel originally created for the human body by our designer to thrive on; it's also the best foods and fuel that our body does better with nutritionally.

Its eating food in its most natural state as Mother Nature provides us. I believe that the problems some people have such as allergies with certain natural foods are to do with the toxins contained in the foods and not the foods themselves, also if a particular food is hybrid or GMO, not as found in nature, this can also cause allergies and huge problems in the body.

We have come so far from what our ancestors knew and ate that people think it's weird to talk about eating a raw food diet, but we are not talking about raw meat, we are talking about natural raw vegetables, legumes, soaked nuts, sprouted soaked seeds that can be prepared into delicious dishes, and is by far the healthiest because of the living enzymes needed by the body. Although it's even better to eat a whole raw food such as a few apples, melons, or cucumbers etc. individually.

Raw foods are low in bad fat, high in fibre, full of the nutrients, minerals, enzymes and amino acids the body needs, and it's the perfect balanced diet. Again when harvested as close from nature as possible. If you consume mainly animal products, you will also benefit from adding a proportion of raw food to your diet daily.

Also, there is no calorie counting because there are no weight gain problems on this diet, it's actually a lifestyle of going back to nature rather than a diet. You may want to count the calories if you need to gain weight, just to make sure you're eating enough of it to maintain your weight and energy levels. The body recognises nutrition more than calories. People on a raw food diet rarely get sick as long as they do it correctly. Raw whole foods were eaten for thousands of years before fire was discovered, and then began the cooking of food and following that, was disease of the body, which got worse with the introduction of processed foods filled with chemicals and toxins.

The lifespan of our ancestors living on this diet was much longer than we live today; they had no chronic conditions or obesity, unlike the rest of the world. When man added meat to his diet, it reduced his lifespan considerably. When man added processed foods to his diet, it reduced his lifespan even further. It has been discovered, and it's no miracle that our indigenous relatives that still eat the raw whole food diet can live up to 130 years or above.

Raw food is living food such as natural fruits, vegetables and sprouts, etc. that is completely raw and still contains living enzymes. Life comes from life. Modern raw food diet is a lifestyle promoting no animal products and the consumption of uncooked, unprocessed and often organic and wild foods naturally grown and harvested.

Raw food eaters believe that the greatest health benefits are attained by eating naturally as nature supplies, living off the land without man's interference. Raw food restaurants are becoming more popular these days, as people discover the benefits of raw foods.

When people add more raw foods to their diet, they often see great benefits and healing.

We all have a choice in what we eat, but I do not buy excuses that raw food is not good for everybody, because when I recommend raw foods to someone, regardless of their age, culture or background, as long as its natural and organic, they always get great results and even reversal of conditions because it's a natural staple food for humans. I know that not everyone can do a raw food diet, because they are just not use to it, but everyone will benefit from adding a percentage of raw to his or her diet.

Human beings can only thrive on certain foods. Living foods. I believe this goes for animals too as the animals on a plant-based diet such as hippo's gorillas, tortoise, giraffe's and elephants have a much longer lifespan than meat-eating animals and are also not as aggressive as meat-eating animals.

Raw food does not mean that you eat just fruits and vegetables alone. You have to add the sprouted foods and seeds with essential oils such as flax seed oil, hemp oil, extra virgin cold pressed olive oil and coconut oil, so you get your full spectrum of nutrition such as protein, good carbohydrates and good fats as well as all your vitamins, minerals and amino acids. These oils are better attained through the actual food itself. These good fats also help to burn fat.

You will be surprised to see the many delicious dishes made from raw food. If you have a fast metabolism and are slim and decide to go for a raw food diet, you will also need to include bodybuilding raw foods such as avocado, banana, soaked nuts, sprouted beans and hemp protein powder as well as eating plenty of natural fruits, which are high in good carbs; otherwise, you can look too thin and unhealthy. To gain weight, you also have to make sure that you eat enough food on a daily basis as mentioned before.

You can also add fruit and vegetable smoothies to your meals or throughout the day, adding banana or avocado with some hemp protein powder to help you build weight. Working out can also help you build weight. Always speak to an expert before you decide to go into something you have not done before.

If you're a person that needs to lose weight, you will be surprised as to how much weight you can lose from this way of eating. And the weight loss will be automatic. The body knows what to do with this type of food; it will clean out the body of accumulated waste.

I had been trying all my life to put on weight and could not, and when I started to eat raw foods, I became even thinner because I was not eating enough and was not happy about the weight loss, but when I started doing regular cleanses and started to eat the correct bodybuilding foods just mentioned, as well as eating enough foods, especially natural fruits and exercising, I began to gain weight as I was able to absorb the nutrients I needed to build up my body. But being naturally slim and not able to eat too much food, I find I can only get to a certain level of weight.

But also when I found out about internal parasites, it made sense; I had always suspected that this may be the reason for me not being able to gain weight, then I discovered information that confirmed that parasites eat your food and the best nutrition before your body can use it to benefit you, I was so not pleased when I discovered this.

Now I try not to give them a chance to get a foothold. I do regular cleanses that includes parasite cleanses to make sure that "I" get to eat my food! I keep my system as clean as possible so that it is very unattractive for parasites to even want to stay. And, by the way, everybody has parasites, and you can still get parasites on a raw food diet, but more so with meats and fish, especially raw fish and pork.

A raw food diet does not include raw animal products such as raw milk and raw cheese, although this is said to have some benefits to certain groups of people, but raw food still gives you everything in balance if you include the correct foods. If you need to lose weight, you do not constantly have to watch what you eat on a raw food diet. You automatically reduce and remain your perfect weight if you keep it up.

A common question on a raw diet is where do you get your protein? I discovered recently that the whole protein thing is just a myth. The biggest animals on the planet, such as gorillas, hippos, elephants, horses, cows etc. only eat leaves, grass, nuts and berries, so how is it that they are so big and strong and live long lives, and where do they get their protein from if protein is so important?

If you still buy into the protein myth, then you can have hemp protein or quinoa, this is a seed that tastes very much like rice and cooks the same way; it can also be sprouted and eaten raw, there is more protein in quinoa than meat. Quinoa also contains all essential amino acids. Other vegan sources of protein are Avocado, Kale, Hemp seeds, Spirulina, Chia seeds, Almonds, Spinach, Broccoli, peas, lentils and chickpeas.

Raw food diet is easier to do when you live in a hot climate as we are all sub-tropical creatures that do far better in the sun and benefit greatly from vitamin D. But if you live in a cold climate, you may need some warm food or soup in the winter months, but these can still be vegan ingredients.

A good compromise that would benefit your health would be 80% raw, and 20% cooked, or even just 50/50 if it's constantly too cold. Ginger and cayenne pepper are very warming to the body if you do not want to eat cooked foods, plus some raw is better than none. And another good thing about a raw diet is that there is some preparation time as in cooked foods, but there is no cooking time, so it is much quicker to prepare your food and saves time.

Constantly eating overcooked vegetarian foods or foods you may consider to be healthy, without any raw living foods in your diet can still lead to sickness because as mentioned earlier, overcooking kills the nutrition in the food and changes the chemical structure of the food to a form that the body can no longer recognise or handle constantly. So it's a good idea not to overcook your food and to include some living foods if you want a good level of health.

Vegan Diet

The vegan diet is also plant-based, just like the raw food diet. This way of eating has also been known to reverse chronic conditions. In a vegan diet, there are no animal products such as meat and dairy products either, and it consists of mainly fruits, vegetables, nuts, seed, grain, legumes and essential fats.

The only difference is that a vegan diet consists of both raw and cooked vegan foods. Vegans, not very often but may occasionally feel tired if they eat too many overcooked foods by not getting the nutrients that are killed off when the food is cooked using very high temperature

And again, as long as you add your bodybuilding foods as we listed in the raw food diet as well as working out, you will not lose too much weight if you don't need to. But if you need to lose the weight, don't worry, you will.

Vegetarian Diet

A vegetarian diet is mainly plant-based raw and cooked foods and consists of the above vegan diet such as fruits, vegetables, nuts, seeds, grain legumes, etc. However, some vegetarians eat processed foods made from flour and animal products such as egg and dairy products whilst others do not eat eggs or dairy products but may eat flour products. Other vegetarians may eat egg but no other dairy products. I remember once in Spain I ordered a vegetarian meal from a restaurant that came with chicken. In Spain if you say you're a vegetarian it means that you don't eat red meat, but you eat chicken and fish. So you have to say vegano and not vegetarian, otherwise you will get animal products.

A vegetarian diet is healthier than a meat diet, but again eating cooked foods above 109 degrees, changes the structure of the food and begins to deplete the living enzymes contained within, and processed foods defeats the whole purpose of being a healthy vegetarian because you may not eat meat or other flesh foods, but the processed foods are just as harmful to your body or worse and some contain hidden meat product such as gelatine and meat flavours.

Pasteurised dairy products are also very mucus forming and can lead to mucus related ailments such as sinus problems, allergies, asthma, etc. This is why some vegetarians still get sick and suffer from mucus-related conditions when they eat pasteurised dairy products as well as conditions linked to processed foods and drinks.

Animal Product Diet

The main modern diet consists of meat, fish, dairy products, sugar, processed dead foods and fatty foods from bad fats. We saw before that when man added meat and these other products into his diet we started to see a progressive decline in health.

As we see today, eating the normal standard diet comes at a serious price of chronic conditions. Maybe it's because in the case of meat, the moment any flesh dies, it begins to decompose and toxins and gases are released into your system as you eat it, whether the meat is cooked thoroughly or not. Meat takes up to three days to pass through your digestive system; meanwhile releasing toxins and gases into your body. So if you're a meat eater you may do well and help yourself by reducing it to a few times a week and not every day.

This is not to mention the deliberate toxins such as nitrates, antibiotics and growth hormones added to the meat to make them grow bigger and faster. Meat is what most people have been brought up on, it was not as bad for our great grandparents as it is for us today as the animal products they ate were from grass fed animals and without the toxic chemicals and hormones.

We've heard so many times while growing up that we should eat our meat because we need the protein to build us up. But the evidence we see today from eating too much meat is serious health problems. When you grow up in a certain society and environment, you believe everything your elders tell you, you have no reason not to because most of the time they can only pass on what they have been taught, whether it's your parents, grandparents, your doctor or your teacher.

It's not easy to leave behind what we have become accustomed to, especially when it comes to our food, our taste buds have taken our whole lifetime to develop and are sometimes stronger than our willpower. But Rome was not built in a day; it may take time to change your diet unless you need to for health reasons. As in my case, it did not take much time at all for me to change my diet because of the immediate health benefits I saw and felt. For me, this was a no-brainer and it has kept me very well and out of hospital for years.

In the promotion of protein in this way of eating, remember that the biggest and strongest animals on the planet are all on a raw vegan diet and they live for years. They get all their protein, calcium and other essential nutrients they need from the raw natural plant-based foods they eat. There is more protein and calcium in some raw food sources than in meat and milk, contrary to what we have been taught.

The cow that provides the milk containing calcium is getting most of its calcium from the grass. So drinking pasteurised and homogenised milk for calcium means you are getting your calcium second-hand and diluted as the process uses heat so kills off most of the calcium. If you want to drink milk, you are better off with raw milk if you can find it.

The Moringa I mentioned earlier has far more protein and calcium than meat and milk. So the recommendation that we need to eat meat for our protein and drink milk for our calcium, I believe is based on mainstream propaganda to get more sales. Just do the test on yourself, cut out hormone fed meat and pasteurised milk for a month or more, replace them with an alternative option and note the difference in your health and vitality.

We will talk more about this later, but, in fact, according to recent studies, when humans consume animal milk that has been pasteurised and homogenised it actually pulls calcium from the bones. Complete opposite to what we have been told, maybe that's why there are so many increased cases of osteoporosis and other bone diseases more than ever, especially in the elderly that have been consuming these products over a longer period. But remember, please don't just take what I am saying, do your own research on everything to be informed with the truth and do the tests on yourself to see how your body responds and how you feel.

It may be a challenge at first, but the struggle and war is generally with the taste buds.

This is further confirmed in that some pets that are fed the modern diet by their owners also often develop some of these same chronic conditions and begin to get grey hairs also as they age.
When I recommend that people cut out the foods and drinks below linked to the common chronic conditions for a week or two, they always come back with incredible results of how they feel and some even inform of conditions that have been reversed.

Below is a list of the common foods linked to the common chronic conditions of today, some or all of which most people consume daily.

These foods are causing accumulation, lack of circulation, dirty thick, sticky stagnant blood, and lack of oxygen that is leading to an acidic and inflamed body, leading to ailments such as blocked arteries, clogged organs, chronic disease and premature death. And these are all very addictive foods.

White Sugar and artificial Sweeteners

The average person consumes over 100 lbs. of refined and artificial sugars each year. This includes sugars that are hidden in processed packaged foods and drinks. Sugar is used as an additive in many packaged foods such as ketchup and baked beans. In packaged foods, sugar can take the form of glucose, dextrose, sucrose, or high-fructose corn syrup.

Artificial sweeteners in diet and other drinks are not even a food but pure chemicals that are 300-500 times sweeter than refined sugar according to Dr Johnson. The artificial sweetener Aspartame has been linked as a cancer-causing substance, but yet is still found in many drinks and foods.

Sugar is basically concentrated crystallised poison and acid to the body and affects your Ph. balance, which causes your blood and other organs to become more acidic leading to disease. Excess acid in the blood will eventually be stored in the fat cells making it difficult to lose weight. The more acidic your body is, the more susceptible you are to disease. The body uses sugar as a drug; it's extremely addictive, puts a huge strain on the organs and destroys the body.

Refined sugar and artificial sweeteners have many detrimental effects on your body. Many people worry about ageing not realising that all that sugar they are consuming is ageing them faster than any other processed food substance.
The pancreas responsible for producing insulin, can only process and burn up natural sugars, so processed or artificial sugars contribute to diabetes by going straight to the blood, spiking your

sugar levels, and over time it will damage your pancreas and lead to diabetes.

Sugar impairs the mineral balance in your body. Essential calcium is pulled from your bones, teeth and tissues to neutralise the consumption of acid sugary substances leading to osteoporosis and brittle bones, suppressing your immune system, lowering your body's natural defences and creating imbalances in your hormones. Sugar clogs your arteries because unused glucose becomes saturated fat and bad cholesterol, which stores in your arteries, leading to high blood pressure and clotting, which can in turn result in stroke and heart attack.

Other conditions affected by a high sugar diet are: Arthritis, Alzheimer's, Parkinson's, Headaches, Cancer, Stomach gas, Intestinal gas, Heart disease, Psoriasis, Weight gain as it turns to fat in the body, PMS, Candida, Tooth decay, Multiple Sclerosis, Inflammation, Cataracts, Gallstones, Bowel disease, Kidney stones, Cystic fibrosis and Depression. Sugar fuels bacteria, viruses, parasites, fungus, mould, yeast and cancer cells, all these are fed by processed sugar and artificial sweeteners.

Healthier Alternatives

Raw, unprocessed honey such as Manuka honey, Stevia, unprocessed raw agave nectar (difficult to find), coconut sugar (make sure nothing else is added), grade B or C maple syrup and date syrup are healthier alternatives. All these are natural sweeteners without any added artificial sugar or toxic ingredients. All can be found in a good health food shop.

Honey such as raw unprocessed or Manuka honey has great health benefits. Honey is very sweet so limit what you eat and make sure it's raw and unprocessed.

Stevia is a natural sweetener made from the stevia plant. Stevia is calorie free and can be found in most health food shops. Make sure your stevia product is natural and does not contain Maltodextrin. Make sure to monitor your own body's response to any new product you may use.

Agave nectar or agave syrup, is a sweetener used in food and drinks. It is often used as a substitute for sugar, syrups, honey and molasses and as an alternative sweetener. Only buy if it's raw and unprocessed; otherwise, it's just a fructose syrup manufactured in a laboratory that has a very high fructose content with no nutritional value and can give you all the above symptoms as found in sugar.

Coconut palm sugar

Coconut palm sugar is made from the flower and sap of the coconut; it contains a fibre called Inulin, which can slow glucose absorption. Coconut sugar is said to have a lower glycemic index than regular table sugar and retains quite a bit of the nutrients found in the coconut palm but is higher in calories than other natural sugars so you may want to reduce the amount you use.

Date syrup

Date syrup as a sweetener can be made very easily by soaking soft, natural pitted dates in filtered water overnight and placing them in a blender with the water the following morning and blending until smooth. Use less water to create a thicker paste. You can also now purchase date syrup from a health food shop.

Maple syrup

Maple syrup is made from the sap of the maple tree, make sure it is real maple syrup and not just maple flavoured syrup, it comes in different grades such as A, B and C; the higher the grade, the darker the colour. B and C are thought to have more nutritional content such as calcium, potassium, zinc, iron and manganese.

White Processed Flour

White processed flour and white flour products such as cakes, biscuits, doughnuts, white pasta, pizza, bagels, etc. This also goes for all types of man-made grain, brown and wholemeal flour. The addiction to bread as a staple diet for most people is causing havoc in their body because most people are gluten intolerant so cannot properly digest it, causing all sorts of gut conditions. Many reverse this just by cutting out bread from their diet.

White and many other flours contain gluten that becomes a sticky paste when mixed with water. Just like glue. I actually remember making glue with flour and water when I was at school. This sticky, gluey substance when eaten in the form of bread, pizza, cakes, biscuits, doughnuts, and white pasta (all the yummy stuff right?) does not change when it enters the body. So accumulation happens in the body leading to aching and stiff joints as it glues everything together. Even so-called brown bread and wholemeal bread has been bleached and depleted of nutrition.

Chlorine gas is used to bleach the flour. In this process, a by-product called alloxan is created that actually destroys beta cells in the pancreas responsible for making insulin. It destroys the insulin-producing function of the pancreas, allowing glucose levels to shoot sky-high. So bleached white processed flour and wholemeal flour can also damage your pancreas.

Consuming white flour products clogs the body and can raise blood pressure levels; it also has the same effect on your blood sugar as eating processed table sugar as it converts to sugar in the body.

Nowadays, you may notice soy flour in certain foods, avoid this as this is likely to be genetically modified (GMO) about 90% of soy products are GMO.

Healthier alternatives.

Sprouted bread, which is raw but tastes as if it's been baked. You can also make your own grain-free bread using almond meal or soaked seeds and nuts. Research how to make alternative grain free bread on the Internet; there are lots of great recipes out there. (These alternative breads are great for those that are gluten intolerant or for those that love bread in general and feel you cannot give it up.)

Dangerous Drinks

Soft drinks and concentrated fruit juices are loaded with artificial sugars and other chemicals that raise your blood sugar.

Coffee and tea contain caffeine that is an external stimulant, so the body will always become dependent on it. This is the reason you get a headache when you have not had your caffeine fix. Studies have shown that caffeine also pulls calcium from the bones and depletes the body of vital Magnesium and Vitamin C. So you would do well to supplement these to replace them. There are some healthy coffees out there so you can do your research if you're a coffee lover.

Diet drinks containing artificial sugars contain more sugar than non-diet drinks.
For years, soft drinks companies have been selling products with ingredients that we now know are linked to a host of conditions such as diabetes, obesity, and kidney stones. These are effects of products that contain High Fructose Corn Syrup and phosphoric acid found in some conventional soft drinks, despite the fact that these drink products are extremely harmful to human health, they are still allowed to be sold to the public.

Healthier alternatives

Freshly squeezed homemade fruit juice, or juices bought from the supermarkets that are not from concentrates and do not have any added sugar; they still may be pasteurised using heat for shelf life, so fresh is always best. Dandelion Coffee and Herbal teas, fruit teas and hot chocolate from raw unprocessed and unsweetened cacao or carob powder are a great alternative for tea and coffee.

Red Meat and Hormone fed Chicken

Red meat is decomposing flesh that stays in the body for a long time before digested. As soon as something is killed, it immediately starts to decompose and release toxins and gases that affect your body when eaten. Also, it takes up to three days or longer for red meat to pass through your system; if you have a digestive system that is impaired, the meat can stay in the gut undigested for decades. It becomes like tar and sticks to the wall of the colon because of the impaired digestive system often caused by eating too many processed and dead foods.

Red meat often contains poisonous toxins such as nitrates and antibiotics as well as growth hormones.
Chicken contains growth hormones that mimic oestrogen, causing all sorts of female problems such as young girls growing breasts early and starting their periods much earlier than normal. Some women find it difficult in conceiving because of an imbalance of too much oestrogen in their body. Male reproductive problems such as erectile dysfunction and lower sperm count are often a result of too much man-made oestrogen from the growth hormones as well as other common toxins people are consuming unawares. As mentioned before, what we are eating today is not the same as what our grandparents ate. It's not so much about not eating this or that, but rather finding out what it contains and what it's doing to your body.

Other dangers linked to meat: saturated fats, cancer forming, and diabetes because of the fat, mucus forming, and deceleration of the metabolic system, fermentation, acidity and putrefying (rotting) in the stomach, constipation and other bowel conditions we see increasing every year.

*Farmed fish** contain toxin and chemicals and are linked to many health problems. If you do eat fish, make sure its wild fish caught in the natural way and not bred in a fish farm, although it may still contain mercury and other toxins. Most fish sold in supermarkets are farmed fish. (See the page below on the full story on farmed fish.)

Healthier alternatives

Red meat and hormone and toxin infested meat are best avoided if you want great health. Eating meat without the nitrates, antibiotics, hormones or other chemicals does not guarantee not having adverse effects on your digestive system. Again, go with your own body's response after eating anything.

Pasteurised Dairy Products

Pasteurised and homogenised Dairy products like cheese, cream, ice cream, milk and yogurt can be incredibly unhealthy, and extremely mucus forming. Pasteurised dairy products are the biggest culprit for sinus problems, allergies, asthma, bronchitis, emphysema, pneumonia, irritable bowel syndrome and colitis, etc. All these conditions are related to an accumulation of mucus in different parts of the body causing the area to become acidic and inflamed. This also depletes the immune system.

When the mucus is in the head, the person usually suffers from sinus problems, and if it moves to the chest area, it's usually allergies, asthma, bronchitis, emphysema and pneumonia. Mucus in the bowels is associated with irritable bowel syndrome, colitis and other bowel conditions, and if left untreated can lead to Crohn's disease, where in some serious cases the bowel has to be removed.

But it's all the same excess mucus in different parts of the body causing the area to become inflamed, accompanied with acid and accumulation from undigested food. Very often, the mucus hardens and causes lumps in different parts of the body. Mucus and fat are also related to cellulite.

Dr Johnson identified that the average person carries around 25 pounds of excess mucus every day within their bodies.

Hormones present in animal milk have also been linked to cysts, breast, prostate and testicular cancer. Doing a regular cleanse and eating a plant-based diet is a great way of getting rid of this excess mucus. You can lose a lot of weight just by getting rid of excess mucus around the body.

As mentioned in relation to dairy products, pasteurised milk leaches calcium from the bones, opposite to what we have heard and hormones present in milk are contributing to an oestrogen overload in men and women, which leads to problems with their reproductive systems. I have been told that the IVF fertility clinics are now constantly packed.   If you have this problem, its best starting by cleansing the digestive system along with other organs of the body, this will help to heal and build up the area.

If you have an impaired digestive system, you may want to try wheat grass juice, natural wheatgrass juice can help to build up the digesting system again.

Some believe that as human milk is only for human babies, animal milk should also be only for animal babies and humans should not drink animal milk.   It is said that cows have much shorter intestines so are able to digest casein, the protein in milk while humans have very long intestines so cannot. This is a choice for you to make yourself, again listen to your body.

Other related conditions of pasteurised dairy: breast, prostate and testicular cancers from hormones present in milk. Listeria, Crohn's Disease, Osteoporosis and other bone diseases and Multiple Sclerosis are also linked to the consumption of pasteurised and homogenised dairy products.

Healthier alternatives

Freshly made coconut milk, almond milk, hazelnut milk and hemp milk are all great tasty alternatives to animal milk without the chemicals and hormones.

Alternative cheeses can be made from various nuts such as soaked almonds, olive oil, lemon and probiotics for culturing. You can find plenty of recipes for non-dairy cheese on the Internet.

Farmed fish is now so common that if you bought fish in the supermarket recently or ordered one in a restaurant, chances are it was farm-raised. About the only places you can find wild-caught fish these days are specialty fine-dining seafood restaurants.

These oceanic feedlots, consisting of acres of net-covered pens tethered offshore were once considered a wonderful solution to over-fishing, but the reality is far from it.

It can take up to five kilos of wild fish and Antarctic krill to produce just one kilo of farmed salmon! Rather than solving the problem of over-fishing, fish farms are literally competing with human consumption for what little wild fish there are left. Open cage salmon farms are also decimating natural salmon stocks, and destroy the livelihoods of fisheries across the world.

Fish Farms Breed Disease that Decimate Wild Fish around the World

Conditions at fish farms are like conditions at factory farms everywhere: overcrowded, sickly, infected animals are fed whatever it takes to grow them as large as possible, and in as short a time as possible. But these techniques create disease and the techniques employed cause otherwise near-non-existent disease to spread past the pens into the wild.

The "answer" is to add antibiotics to the fish feed — the identical "safety" measure employed by cattle and poultry farms, for example. As a result of the excessive use of antibiotics, resistant strains of disease have emerged that now infect both wild and domesticated fish.

Sea lice, a type of crustacean that is easily incubated by captive fish on farms, have also become a significant problem. To deal with it, chemicals that have not been tested for safety on other species are now being routinely used in salmon farms — even though no one actually knows what these untested chemicals will do to other crustaceans, such as shrimp, crab and lobster. After all, these pens are in open water, and there's no way to control the spread of these chemicals.

The inevitable result of these modern fish farming practices is an evil circle of disease and antibiotic use, followed by the emergence of antibiotic resistant strains. Diseases created by salmon farms have now destroyed the Chilean fishing industry and affect wild salmon in Canada as well as sea trout in Ireland and Scotland. The wild salmon fisheries in the US have also gone bust.

Farmed Fish Also Pose Additional Human Health Hazards

In addition to being an unsustainable practice and an economic disaster, farm-raised fish can also spell disaster for your health. It's important to understand that ALL farm-raised fish — not just salmon — are fed a concoction of vitamins, antibiotics, and depending on the fish, synthetic pigments, to make up for the lack of natural flesh coloration due to the altered diet. Without it, the flesh of caged salmon, for example, would be an unappetizing, pale grey.

The fish are also fed pesticides, along with compounds such as toxic copper sulphate, which is frequently used to keep nets free of algae. Not only do you ingest these drugs and chemicals when you eat the fish, but these toxins also build up in sea-floor sediments. In this way, industrial fish farming raises many of the same environmental concerns about chemicals and pollutants that are associated with feedlot cattle and factory chicken farms.

In addition, fish waste and uneaten feed further litter the sea floor beneath these farms, generating bacteria that consume oxygen vital to shellfish and other bottom-dwelling sea creatures.
Studies have also consistently found levels of PCBs, dioxins, toxaphene and dieldrin, as well as mercury, to be higher in farm-raised fish than wild fish. This fact alone would be cause to

reconsider consuming farmed fish! Wild caught fish have already reached such toxic levels; it's impossible to recommend eating them with a clear conscience anymore. (**Source: Pure Salmon Champagne**)

For more information on genetically engineered fish and foods, see Seeds of Deception by Jeffrey M. Smith

The idea is to clone everything to increase food production, treating people as human experiments in the process. There is enough food in the world; contrary to what we are told, this is also another myth that the food in the world is running out. An unbelievable amount of food is wasted daily around the world, yet some people are starving.

Consuming GMO fish and other GMO foods comes with problems such as immune system problems, reproductive problems, acceleration of ageing, bad cholesterol and other problems. The goal is to create all the world's food supply using man-made methods as a means of control to increase profits, not caring about the consequences to our health and the environment. But humans can never match Mother Earth in the perfect food she has created for us.

CHAPTER 6

Accumulation of Waste in the Body

Waste in the forms of human waste, mucus, heavy metals, radiation and toxins that are meant to be eliminated from our body on a daily basis are accumulating and remaining in our body.

The waste remains because of processed foods and meats that the body finds difficult to digest and cannot eliminate completely, excess mucus from continuously eating pasteurised dairy or processed soy products, toxins from certain ingredients in our foods and drinks, and toxins we breathe in from our environment. I mentioned earlier that the human body was designed to cleanse itself naturally through certain organs.   This cleansing occurs as we eat living whole foods that are cleansing to the body, especially the natural fruits and vegetables that contain large amounts of water.

Because most people are eating mainly processed foods rather than raw living foods and whole foods, this natural cleansing process is not possible, and as mentioned before, most people walk around with at least 20 pounds or more of excess human waste, mucus and a list of heavy metal and toxic waste building up in their body every day.

Accumulation of Human Waste

Human waste trapped in your digestive system rots, becomes more toxic and decays daily, and this slowly poisons your body. Many people are constipated and are not aware. You can be constipated even if you have one bowel movement per day.

Constipation can make you feel tired, sluggish, bloated, irritated and overweight, and this can go on for so long it begins to seem normal. You don't even realise that the cause is constipation and that it's a serious danger to your health! Chemical laxatives and antacid drugs can often make the problem worse. Healthy digestion and regularity are fundamental to a healthy body. It is said that health begins in the gut. Constipation, diarrhoea, and bloating are serious problems. They often set the stage for even more serious conditions if they go untreated and the colon unregulated.

The average person empties their bowels once every two or three days. Most people do not have the perfect digestive system. The perfect digestive system is supposed to work like this: If you eat three meals a day, you should empty your bowels of waste three times a day and within 30 to 60 minutes after you have eaten, because not everything we eat is taken into the body for energy, there is waste with everything we eat, as with fruits and vegetables the body releases the fibre as waste. But if you eat three meals a day and empty your bowels once a day, you have two lots of waste in your system just sitting there, giving off gas and rotting.

Do the calculations for this over a period of a week to see how much human waste and excess mucus you carry around in your body. You may only realise this when you decide to do a good colon cleanse and experience emptying your bowels several times a day. Is this no wonder why so many people have bowel and colon cancer problems nowadays? But having said that, it is far better to have one bowel movement a day than to go two or more days without. In the worst cases some people can go for weeks, and I have heard about a case where someone had not emptied their bowels for months. This shows you the capacity of the bowel to hold waste.

Accumulation of Mucus

Mucus is the same thing that comes out of the body during a cold. This is the same excess mucus in different parts of the body causing health problems.

Excess mucus is created mainly from two very high mucus forming foods as we saw earlier, which are pasteurised dairy products and processed soy products, the next being red meat. Excess mucus can also be created from eating dried nuts and seeds that do not contain natural oils, without first soaking them first because of enzyme inhibitors that block enzyme function in the nut or seed, which is a natural process of protecting them from insects. So when you soak them it releases the enzyme inhibitors and prevents them from becoming mucus forming. As Doctor Johnson explains, excess mucus leads to many common conditions as seen earlier that the mucus gets into different parts of the body causing different symptoms and given different names but it's the same mucus causing these symptoms and inflammation in different parts of the body. When you eat the right foods and cleanse the body of excess mucus by doing an internal body cleanse specifically to remove the excess mucus, most of these conditions can reverse.

I no longer get colds, where I used to get them all the time in the past, even pneumonia as mentioned when I was on a dead food diet but have not had a cold for many years; maybe it's because I have been doing daily and quarterly cleanses to remove any excess mucus and building my immune system with living foods.

Accumulation of Toxic Waste

- 75,000 synthetic chemicals have been introduced into our environment in the last 70 years
- Only 7% have been tested for safety in humans, most of them you can't see, smell or taste
- Over 3.5 billion kilograms of toxins are released into our environment every year
- We get 10,000 hits of free radicals per day attacking our cells, damaging cells, causing disease and premature ageing.
- Around 106,000 people die each year from correctly prescribed medication.

Toxins and toxic heavy metals negatively impact our health. They are in the air we breathe, the water we drink, the food we eat, the products we use on our skin, and in our homes, the objects we touch and even the fillings in our teeth. Exposure is almost impossible to avoid. Heavy metals such as aluminium, mercury, cadmium, lead and arsenic, etc. build up in the body over time contributing to poor health.

How Toxic is Your Home?

Statistics show that there are more toxic chemicals in our homes than outside our homes due to chemical cleaning products and chemicals on items found in the home. As a result of the chemicals that have been released into the environment, we now live on a toxic planet; there are toxins everywhere, in and outside of us.

We would do well to try and minimise the amount of extra toxins we take into our bodies through what we eat and drink and products we use on our skin and in our homes, such as household sprays and cleaning products, deodorants and cosmetics, this is the only thing we are in control of when it comes to toxins. There are companies that are dedicated to reducing the use of toxic chemicals in our home cleaning, personal care and other products so we do not have to dump chemicals on our skin and in our homes every day.

During my research, I discovered that some of the products that claim to be free of toxins were not completely toxin-free. To be sure, read the ingredients, then find out what the ingredients are and what they do before you allow the product into your home and on your skin. Remember if in doubt keep it out. I use raw virgin coconut oil to cleanse my skin, I also use it on my teeth, hair and internally through my food, and it's natural and amazingly healthy.

One hundred and fifty chemicals found in the average home have been linked to allergies, birth defects, cancer and psychological abnormalities. **(Source: Consumer Product Safety Commission)**

Studies link 50% of all health problems to indoor air quality, which is proven to be 70% more toxic than outdoor pollution if you use chemicals in the home. Environmental studies have shown that four million pounds of chemical cleaners go down the drain annually. Chemical waste causes huge, detrimental toxic effects on our water system. So you see the importance and need to detox our body and our homes regularly.

Because of the level of toxins in and around us, including breathing in toxins from chemtrails in the sky, I think it is important to do simple daily cleanses as well as a deeper cleanse periodically. Some still think that the trails in the sky are from aeroplanes, aeroplane trails disappear quite quickly; chemtrails, on the other hand, hang around for ages and expands while we breathe it in through the air.

There are a few things you can do to cleanse the body of toxins and excess waste on a daily basis. You do not need to do them all at once. Also make sure you do a deeper periodic cleanse.

1. Oil pulling, an ancient method of detoxing the body and building the teeth and gums, by swishing a tablespoon of coconut or sunflower oil around the mouth for 20 minutes then spitting out and brushing your teeth as normal. (Do not swallow.) Best done in the morning before you eat and drink anything. I do it while in the shower to save time.

2. Drink two, 8 oz. glass of water when you wake up
3. Drink warm lemon water in the mornings
4. Juicing fruits and vegetables are great for cleansing
5. Eating natural organic fruits is a natural cleanser
6. Moringa Oleifera, can be added to smoothies or lemon water (good for removing mucus)
7. Diatomaceous Earth (food grade only) good for removing heavy metal and mucus
8. Activated Charcoal (good for removing toxins and food poisoning)
9. Daily exercises. Moving the body helps to shift waste out of the body

10. Research Orgone energy and products for neutralising radiation from phones and other equipment in the home as well as promotion of other health benefits.

Identify Safe and Toxic Plastics

Our homes may be full of toxic plastics, used in many kitchen and household items that can contain a variety of dangerous chemicals.

These toxins can be found in plastic food packaging, plastic food storage containers, plastic water bottles, canned foods, toys, cooking utensils and even kitchen appliances and many other household products.   Using plastics to store our food, leaches chemicals into the food and drinks we consume. These toxins are extremely dangerous to our health and most dangerous of all to unborn babies and toddlers.

It is important to recognise the good plastics from the bad ones. The easiest way to identify toxic plastic is by referring to the recycling codes above. Below is a list of some common plastics used. Look out for a number in a triangle under the plastic container such as the ones above. If possible, store your food in glass dishes and jars.

Plastic 1 – PETE or PET (Polyethylene Terephthalate)

- Picked up by most curbside recycling programs, plastic 1 is usually clear and used to make soda and water bottles. Some consider it safe, but this plastic is known to allow bacteria to accumulate.
- It's found mostly in soda bottles, water bottles, beer bottles, salad dressing containers, mouthwash bottles, and peanut butter containers.
- Plastic #1 is recycled into tote bags, furniture, carpet, paneling, fiber, and polar fleece.
-

Plastic 2 – HDPE (High Density Polyethylene)

- Plastic 2 is typically opaque and picked up by most curbside recycling programs. This plastic is one of the 3 plastics **considered to be safe**, and has a lower risk of leaching.
- It's found mostly in milk jugs, household cleaner containers, juice bottles, shampoo bottles, cereal box liners, detergent bottles, motor oil bottles, yogurt tubs, and butter tubs like jugs, detergent bottles, juice bottles, butter tubs, and toiletries bottles are made of this. It is usually opaque. This plastic is considered safe and has low risk of leaching.
- Plastic 2 is recycled into pens, recycling containers, picnic tables, lumber, benches, fencing, and detergent bottles, to name a few.

Plastic 3 – V or PVC (Vinyl)

- Plastic 3 is used to make food wrap, plumbing pipes, and detergent bottles, and is seldom accepted by curbside recycling programs. These plastics used to, and still may, contain phthalates, which are linked to numerous health issues ranging from developmental problems to miscarriages. They also contain DEHA, which can be carcinogenic with long-term exposure. DEHA has also been linked to loss of bone mass and liver problems. Don't cook with or burn this plastic.

- It's found in shampoo bottles, clear food packaging, cooking oil bottles, medical equipment, piping, and windows.
- This plastic is recycled into paneling, flooring, speed bumps, decks, and roadway gutters.
-

Plastic 4 – LDPE (Low Density Polyethylene)

- Low density polyethylene is most found in squeezable bottles, shopping bags, clothing, carpet, frozen food, bread bags, and some food wraps. Curbside recycling programs haven't been known to pick up this plastic, but more are starting to accept it. Plastic 4 rests among the recycling symbols **considered to be safe**.
- This plastic is recycled into compost bins, paneling, trash can liners and cans, floor tiles, and shipping envelopes.
-

Plastic 5 – PP (Polypropylene)

- Increasingly becoming accepted by curbside recycle programs, plastic 5 is also **one of the safer plastics** to look for.
- It is typically found in yogurt containers, ketchup bottles, syrup bottles, and medicine bottles.
- Polypropylene is recycled into brooms, auto battery cases, bins, pallets, signal lights, ice scrapers, and bicycle racks.
-

Plastic 6 – PS (Polystyrene)

- Polystyrene is Styrofoam, which is notorious for being difficult to recycle, and thus, bad for the environment. This kind of plastic

also poses a health risk, leaching potentially toxic chemicals, especially when heated. Most recycling programs won't accept it.
- Plastic 6 is found in compact disc cases, egg cartons, meat trays, and disposable plates and cups.
- It is recycled into egg cartons, vents, foam packing, and insulation. (**source: Natural Science**)
These chemicals have also been found to make fibroids and other growths bigger as well as causing problems with hormone balance that leads to other conditions such as infertility in men and women.

You can protect yourself from these chemicals by eating foods that are high in phytonutrients to counteract the effects. Foods that are high in phytonutrients are cruciferous vegetables such as Spinach, Onions, Kale, Broccoli, Cauliflower, Cabbage and Brussels sprouts.

Blunders in hospitals are linked to
90,000 patient deaths a year

As many as 90,000 patient deaths a year could be linked to hospital errors, according to a study published. One in ten NHS patients is harmed while in the hospital and up to half of all blunders could be avoided, researchers found. Of those who are harmed, around one in ten errors may have contributed to the patient's death.

The alarming rate of 'adverse events' is revealed in a study of patients admitted to a large teaching hospital in the North of England. Nationally, it could mean that 900,000 patients going into hospital each year suffer damage from errors including injury, infection, poor diagnosis and inadequate care.
Among the problems identified are:

Hospital acquired infections such as MRSA;

Complications during or after surgery;

Wrong diagnoses;

Pressure ulcers;

Drug complications;

Falls;

Unplanned transfers to operating theatre and intensive care;

Unplanned readmissions.

Over 750,000 people actually die in the United States every year, not from accidents, but they die from something far more common and rarely perceived by the public as dangerous: Modern medicine. (**Source: Daily Mail 2007**)

According to the ground breaking 2003 medical report Death by Medicine, by Drs. Gary Null, Carolyn Dean, Martin Feldman, Debora Rasio and Dorothy Smith, 783,936 people in the United States die every year from conventional medicine mistakes.

CHAPTER 7

Return To Mother Nature

Returning back to the basics of what she has provided us through nature is the key to our health, why return to Nature to create our health? The simple truth is that we have been given everything we needed before time and in nature we will find many answers and solutions to our questions. Our designer has provided the best fuel our body needs to run smoothly.

We did not have the complicated and ingenious task of creating natural herbs, fruits and vegetables; it was all done for us. We were also given organs that can take care of themselves as long as we give our body the correct fuel to help this process.

Mother Nature made provisions for us from nature before we existed. There is information in living foods that correspond to our body, these original natural foods work synergistically with our body, but when we put artificial dead foods in our body, the body cannot recognise that information or correspond with it so treats it as a foreign object and eventually these toxins throw everything out of balance, so the body begins to deteriorate.

The human body was originally built to last for hundreds of years and when you read ancient accounts of history, people lived for a few hundred years at a time and 120 years was considered still young. We read earlier that our ancestors lived well over a hundred years and so do the cultures that still observe the natural laws of nature today.

The chronic and toxic conditions of today did not exist. When we began to consume man-made foods and forced to breathe in pollution, it cut the lifespan of mankind drastically, and as we all know, not many people live much beyond 100 except for our indigenous relatives who still eat off the land as Mother Nature provides it.   So this means that even though we have various toxins around us if we stick to the original diet, cleanse the body and live in a stress-less condition, it is possible to live to 120 years and beyond.

When people ate natural foods as nature intended, there was no slaughtering of animals, animals are more intelligent than we give them credit for; an animal knows when it's about to be slaughtered and takes on a lot of fear, stress and pain, it is possible to take on that same fear, pain and stress as you consume them.

Also, there were no processed foods around, no preservatives except for natural salts, and no man-made chemicals and toxins. There was only one way of growing and harvesting food, and that was the natural way without chemicals, toxic pesticides or GMOs. The ground and soil were rich and not depleted of essential minerals. All of this reflected in a healthy, long life, peaceful and slow ageing process without sickness. People did not get sick because of the foods they ate.

People who make the effort to eat as close to nature as possible, eating more living foods and supplementing their diet with plant-based supplements or products containing chlorophyll tend to have a longer lifespan without the diseases and living to a ripe old age without medication.

Chlorophyll is the blood of the plant and contain living enzymes that works miracles when consumed.

Enzymes are proteins that facilitate chemical reactions in living organisms, and they are required for every single chemical reaction that takes place in your body. Enzymes run all your tissues, muscles, bones, organs and cells, which is the life force of the food that gives life to your body.

Our lifespan is directly related to depletion of our enzyme potential. The use of supplemental food enzymes helps to decrease the rate of depletion, resulting in a longer, healthier life and vitality. So Enzymes equals Life.

Today's Challenges

We have major soil depletion from the lack of minerals and toxic chemicals in the soil as well as green harvesting of our foods. There are also more and more chemicals and toxic ingredients being added to our environment, food and drinks.

I also mentioned that a major part of the food chain is processed or has been tampered with, mass-produced and sold to the unsuspecting public, who put their trust in the food industry and expect good food.

I'm sure that if you had the chance to speak to a large corporate farmer that produces chemical, toxic, antibiotic and hormone-laden meat and dairy products, you would find although they supply it for human consumption, I'm sure they and their families are not consuming it themselves because they are aware of what's in it.

But this is how they make their living, along with the pressure of demand and having to produce the food in a certain way to meet government rules and regulations, although we all know that chemicals injected into animals is not to benefit the end consumer. But they will continue to manufacture and sell it to the public, who are prepared to eat it because they trust the companies they are buying from and trust that the government is looking out for their health and safety.

The same is that if you were to speak to a manufacturer of prescription drugs, most of them are prepared to manufacture and sell their products to the public, but they and their families will not take it because they know what's in it and the damaging effects on the body. But they are profiting hugely from this, so they will continue to manufacture and sell it to the public who have been told to consume them for their condition. I think it's time to wake up!

This is why we need to do our own research. It's so important to read the ingredients on labels so we know what we are putting in our body and not just trust that the manufacturers will do that for us.

So to put it bluntly, you see that the health problems we have today started as a result of manipulations and corporate greed and people who are prepared to do anything to make money, no matter the cost to others. People's lives are of very little value nowadays, profit comes before lives, and this is a big shame. Let us take control of our own health and life, and then we will not be victims of deception that allows others to profit from our misery.

The Healing of the Nations

"The leaves of the tree were for the healing of the Nations"

This quote above comes from Revelation 22:2 and gives a big clue in how we can get well through the miracle healing power of herbs. Nobody needs to suffer and die prematurely; we just need to go back to basics and use the herbs and consume the correct fuel that is available in order to survive this toxic onslaught.

If you speak to an experienced herbalist, he or she will tell you that there is virtually a herb or combination of herbs that can heal virtually every disease known to man. Why do you not hear about this?

You do not hear about this in mainstream because natural herbs cannot be patented, plus there is not a lot of money to be made for the big corporations in healing people with herbs because they grow everywhere, and these companies normally fund the advertisements and big publicity campaigns. People who take their time to research other alternative methods are seeing a reversal of conditions such as cancer, diabetes, heart disease, even Aids and other so-called incurable diseases. Yet we hear so often about research to find a cure for certain chronic diseases, hmmm!

The truth is there is more profit in keeping people ignorant and sick rather than healing people with the natural herbs that Mother Nature has provided for the healing of the Nations.
There is no profit in getting people well.
This is why we need to wake up and take control of our own health because nobody is looking out for your health, you are the only one that can do that.

About four years ago, a friend showed me a promotional drink from Cancer Research UK. When we looked at the ingredients in this drink being given away as a promotional item, one of the top ingredients was Aspartame, and then sugar.

I was absolutely outraged when I saw this as it's now public knowledge that the artificial sweetener Aspartame is linked as a cancer-causing ingredient, and sugar is known to feed cancer. I would have thought that as they have been researching for years for a cure for cancer, surely they would have come across this well-known fact by now? Or at least come across all the other natural cures out there now for cancer and other chronic conditions.

I contacted them about their promotional drink and was told by the receptionist that they would pass my query on. I did not hear anything for about a month, so I emailed them and have not heard anything since.

Many people are healing themselves of cancer, but you don't hear this in mainstream news, only in the alternative news channels and social media where people can share their real life alternative healing stories.   Many others have also healed themselves by allowing the body to cleanse and rebalance itself by changing to a vegan diet.

This is one of the reasons why I cannot stress enough that people need to stay informed and educate themselves rather than completely putting their lives and their families' lives in the hands of other people who may not have their best interest in mind.

There are countless testimonials from people who have cut out certain foods like meat, processed and sugary products and used simple cleansing and nourishing and have seen incredible results and even reversal of conditions. So this proves to me that sickness is not a mystery, it just takes common sense knowledge.

The leaves of the tree are truly for the healing of the nations, but unless you know this and apply it, it cannot help you.

Healthier Choices

Most of us have been raised on the common foods linked to the common chronic conditions we saw earlier. Our parents may not have realised the impact these foods can have on our health as they slowly crept into our lives and onto our dinner tables and plates mainly as a result of advertising campaigns. Maybe you did not realise the impact these foods have on your health before reading this book. But we see it all around us with increased obesity and increased chronic diseases and far too many people dying before their time.

This is a tragedy that nobody can deny. It will only stop when people start to re-educate themselves about food and eating medicinal foods that heal the body and mind rather than the deadly foods that kill the body and mind.

This book is not to tell you what you should or should not eat, it is simply written to alert, inform, educate and point out the dangers of dead processed foods and toxic ingredients compared to the life in living foods, so that you can make your own informed choices. I am still learning and discovering things every day, and it's my hope that as we get more educated and share the information that we learn, we will one day see a huge reduction or even better, an end to people around us dying of a common chronic condition that could have been prevented or even reversed.

I know that it is not always easy to eat the correct diet with our busy schedules and lifestyle. And with all the different conflicting information out there, it can get confusing. But you cannot go wrong if you stick to real food, as natural as possible and not man-made food.

Eating healthy is practical, and you have to start somewhere. If you feel you have to eat certain foods, make sure it's the best and does not contain any additives with chemicals, toxins, antibiotics or hormones, otherwise bad health will naturally follow. A chronic condition showing up as a result of the consumption of the dangerous foods list is sadly inevitable because the body was not made to carry toxins permanently within.

Prevention is better than cure as we all know, but if you feel something is wrong, it is a good idea to go and get it checked out as soon as possible before it gets worse.
You will have to make the decision to see a naturopath or begin cleansing the body with living foods or go to the doctor and hospital that will possibly have you on toxic drugs, making your body more toxic and masking the symptoms and possibly one drug after the other probably for the rest of your life, or until it cuts your life short. Please don't let this happen to you or your family members, it's too painful when you have seen many family members and friends die around you due to a diet-related chronic condition that could have been prevented or even reversed. If the recommendation from the doctor is that you take medication, make sure you do what you can to build your immune system through a healthy whole food diet that will cleanse your body of the toxins at the same time. When the living foods begin to heal your body, then you can discuss with your doctor to slowly begin the reduction of the medication until you do not need them anymore.

I completely understand that when someone is first diagnosed with a serious condition, you may get scared and very vulnerable and susceptible to a doctor's directions, drugs and medical procedures. But remember the choice is always yours. Don't allow fear to force you into anything.

And the best thing to do at this stage is to stop putting more dead foods in your system that will make the situation worse and try to get your body back into balance. Then start following a daily diet of living foods, starting with daily juicing of vegetable and fruit juice to help your body to begin to cleanse and heal itself. You can juice many times a day, but make sure you are juicing natural, non-toxic vegetables, especially the dark green leafy vegetables; you can add one or two fruits such as apple, orange juice or pear to make it more palatable.

If you find a change of diet difficult to do, which you may do as the foods that are bad for us are very addictive due to the chemical content and toxins, what you can do is just start by eliminating one bad food at a time or one group of bad foods such as fizzy drinks one week, replacing it with a natural alternative drink or juices, replacing pasteurised milk with almond or any other nut milk, hemp milk, or healthier options, then go on from there replacing what you are eating with healthier alternatives. But if you have a chronic condition, you need to stop these bad foods immediately and concentrate on healing your body with living foods and cleansing.

Another great way to start is by learning how to make some delicious healthier alternatives that would make you feel that you don't want to go back to the bad stuff anymore. It's not always easy, and it may take time and discipline to eat healthy, but this is your health we are talking about, and the rewards will be long-lasting and very visible to you and to others.

We hear often about a balanced diet, your diet can only be balanced nutritionally when the foods you eat are living, natural foods and not processed. You cannot get a balanced diet on processed foods as there is no nutrition in it to balance. With more and more health food shops and cafes opening up, there is an increase of healthier and better choices opening up around us.

Before I eat anything, I think to myself, is this good for me? Will it bring health and life to my body? Or is it just dead food that will leave a negative mark in my body and take life out of my body? I try not to let my eyes or my stomach dictate my choices anymore. Having a strong willpower helps. Enjoy your food but just know what you're eating. It's not just about what you put into your body, but also what comes out is equally important.

At the end of this book, I have given you some yummy recipes for great tasting healthy, vegan and raw living foods that I have put together for you. I have compiled living, enzyme-rich, oxygen-rich foods into breakfast, lunch and dinner menus with added healthy smoothies, juices and desserts.

Yes, there is such a thing as healthy desserts! I call them guilt-free desserts. There is also a chart in this book giving some examples of healthy grains and seeds that I have used in some of my recipes. If you do go on a health journey, it will be like starting an aspect of your life all over again, but it can also be exciting too, especially when you start seeing and feeling the benefits and great results from cleansing the body, it will encourage you to continue.

When looking for a cleansing program, make sure the ingredients are natural organic and gentle on the stomach. The organs that need to be cleansed are the colon, liver and gallbladder, kidneys/bladder, lymphatic system and blood. All vital organs need to be cleansed of accumulated waste such as human waste, excess mucus, parasites, worms, toxins, radiation and heavy metals.

Drinking plenty of good structured, living or filtered water and eating natural organic fruits and vegetables with a high water content such as watermelon, coconuts, cucumber, celery, apples, pears, peaches, etc. are also very cleansing to the body. But if you have never done a cleanse or detox before, you will most certainly have years of accumulated waste in your body and will need special herbal cleansing products to help shift the waste. Especially if you have been on the traditional standard diet containing the ten dangerous foods.

Be prepared though for a detox effect, this is a reaction that may happen when the toxins are released from your body; some people experience a headache, feel sick, may get flu-like symptoms, dizziness or break outs on the skin or vomiting, etc. It may feel unpleasant for a short while, but it should not last too long, maybe one or two days or less, and when it's over you feel and look great.

Not everybody experiences a detox reaction, it depends what you've been eating before you do the cleanse, but I need to warn you in case you do, so if this does happen to you, don't stop the cleanse, just drink a lot more pure, clean water to help flush the chemicals and toxins out of your body even faster.

Try to continue the cleanse; if you stop and the toxins remain in you, this will inevitably lead to something else, it will not just disappear. Remember that the toxins have been accumulating in your body for your whole lifetime, and it will not come out in a day, it will take time. But you are in for a great treat when it's all over. Stick with it, you will not regret it. The detox reaction is just like a withdrawal symptom, and once you are clean, you feel amazing. But if you have not done this before, it is very important to start off slowly by transitioning to minimise the detox effect by cutting out certain foods one at a time and replacing them as I said before with healthier options. Otherwise, if you get a severe detox effect, you may panic and run to the hospital, which is not a good idea if you want to avoid drugs that will make you even more toxic.

If you choose to do individual cleanses of your organs rather than choosing one product that can clean the entire system, make sure you always start with a colon cleanse because the colon must be clear and in good working order so that all other accumulated waste from the other organs that need to be eliminated through the bowel can do so without any obstructions. Otherwise, if you are constipated and you try and do a liver cleanse, for example, you will have more backed up toxins going back into your system that can make you feel sick.

The key is to get your body back into balance, you do this by not only making sure your organs are in good working order through cleansing but also nourishing and balancing your body by adding the essential vitamins, minerals, nutrients and amino acids and eating more alkaline foods such as fruits and vegetables and avoiding "acid"-forming and accumulating foods such as on the common foods list.

CHAPTER 8

God made food

This article has been circulating the Internet for a while, I don't know where it originates from but it's so remarkable and credit to the person who first discovered it. I found that it's based on an ancient philosophy called the doctrine of signature and that every food looks like the part of the body that it's good for.

God made foods, or the Genesis diet consists of fruit, vegetable, grain, legumes, pulse, nuts, seed, herbs and healthy starches such as soaked beans, peas, lentils, wild rice, essential fats, and so on. We have been given a great clue as to what foods help what part of our body! God's Pharmacy is truly amazing!

A Tomato

Has four chambers and is red. The heart has four chambers and is red. All of the research shows tomatoes are loaded with lycopene and are indeed pure heart and blood food.

Grapes

Hang in a cluster that has the shape of the heart. Each grape looks like a blood cell, and all of the research today shows grapes are also profound heart and blood vitalising food.

A Walnut

Looks like a little brain, a left and right hemisphere, upper cerebrums and lower cerebellums. Even the wrinkles or folds on the nut are just like the neo-cortex. We now know walnuts help develop more than three-dozen neuron-transmitters for brain function.

Kidney Beans

Actually heal and help maintain kidney function, and yes, they look exactly like the human kidneys.

Celery, Bok Choy, Rhubarb

Look just like bones. These foods specifically target bone strength. Bones are 23% sodium and these foods are 23% sodium. If you don't have enough sodium in your diet, the body pulls it from the bones, thus making them weak. These foods replenish the skeletal body.

Avocados, Eggplant and Pears

Target the health and function of the womb and cervix of the female — they look just like these organs. Today's research shows that when a woman eats one avocado a week, it balances hormones, sheds unwanted birth weight, and prevents cervical cancers. And how profound is this — it takes exactly nine (9) months to grow an avocado from blossom to ripened fruit. There are over 14,000 photolytic chemical constituents of nutrition in each one of these foods (modern science has only studied and named about 141 of them)

Figs

Are full of seeds and hang in two's when they grow. Figs increase the mobility of male sperm and increase the numbers of sperm as well to overcome male sterility.

Sweet Potatoes

Look like the pancreas and actually balance the glycemic index of diabetics.

Olives

Assist the health and function of the ovaries and are great for the skin.

Lemons, Limes

And other Citrus fruits look just like the mammary glands of the female and actually assist the health of the breasts and the movement of lymph in and out of the breasts.

Onions

Look like the body's cells. Today's research shows onions help clear waste materials from all of the body cells. They even produce tears, which wash the epithelial layers of the eyes. A working companion, garlic, also helps eliminate waste materials and dangerous free radicals from the body.

As we have seen, there are 2 Types of Foods.
Living Foods and Dead Foods

Dead foods are basically manufactured processed and cooked out foods that have no nutritional value. They are foods that are artificial hybrid and GMO foods that will eventually bring sickness and even premature death to the body, such as the foods on the common foods list. And Living foods are foods provided to us by Mother Nature, full of living enzymes, vitamins, minerals, amino acids and nutrients from fruits, vegetables, herbs, super foods and sprouted foods.

Some healthier alternatives to processed grains

Pasta	Rice	Root vegetables	Sprouted grain	Cereal	Seeds
Quinoa	Black rice	Parsnips	Amaranth	Barley	Sunflower
Buckwheat	Red rice	Turnips	Quinoa	Oats	Hemp
Kamut	Wild rice	Sweet potato	Millet	Millet	Pumpkin
		Yam	Rye	Amaranth	Flax
		Swede	Lentils		Sesame
					Chia
					Alfalfa

131

Remember to soak your seeds, non-oily nuts and grains to bring out the live enzymes and remove the enzyme inhibitors, otherwise they are dead. Remember certain dry nuts such as almonds and cashews and seed can be very mucus forming when not soaked. You do not need to soak nuts that have plenty of natural oils such as walnuts, brazil nuts, pine nuts, pecans and macadamia nuts.

You can find live sprouted foods such as alfalfa sprouts and other sprouted beans and seeds in health food shop or most supermarkets.

Although man-made grain can be deadly, healthy grains as seen in the above chart are important to human survival and an essential part of a healthy balanced diet. Some cereals are also made from grains. But look for cereals that are made from grains found on the chart above. Grains are the seeds of different types of grasses, which are cultivated for food. They come in many shapes and sizes, and can be large or as small as quinoa.

Healthy grains are a good source of good carbohydrates, protein, various vitamins and minerals and are naturally low in fat. Whole-grain that haven't been refined or bleached are a much healthier option.

Culinary Herbs

Culinary herbs are from the leafy green parts of a plant, and spices, from other parts of the plant, including the seeds, berries, barks, roots and fruit. Culinary herbs just like spices, are full of flavour and strong enough to be used in small amounts to provide flavour in food.

Medicinal Herbs

*Medicinal herbs should be used with proper supervision.

Remember that certain herbs such as cayenne pepper, garlic and ginger have natural blood thinning properties, so consult your doctor if you are taking blood thinning medication.

Certain herbs should also be avoided for pregnant and lactating women as they may be too strong for the baby, so remember to consult your doctor

When we have done all we know to make our health better and we find nothing is changing, maybe it's time to go back to the basics of what Mother Nature has already provided us.

Herbs have largely been forgotten by the masses but have been around since time, but they are becoming more popular with people slowly waking up to using herbs to help treat their ailments. The Ancient Egyptians used oils from herbs and seeds for their health benefits. In the past, almost all medicines we took were herbs.

Most of you may not be aware that buying certain herbal remedies has become more difficult as the government restrictions do not allow manufacturers of herbal products to put therapeutic benefits and information on labels. You may ask why this is.

I will leave you to figure that one out yourself, but know that profit always comes before our health when we leave our health to others.

Every now and again, someone will try to report something negative about herbs, yet nobody that I have heard of has ever died from an herb overdose or reaction, and herbs have been around way before man-made drugs that have claimed many lives.

During my research a few years ago, I found that it was estimated that over 200,000 people in the US die each year from adverse reactions to their medication. In the UK, the number was around 114,000. I'm sure those numbers have risen greatly since.

This is one of the reasons why I took the step to take control of my health, and I happy I did. As we have seen, it's actually more profitable to keep you sick and in the dark.

Once you have a certain disease like heart disease or cancer, there is nothing much that medical science can do to reverse this completely without putting you on drugs for the rest of your life. All that can be done is a transplant, put foreign objects in the body, cut out sections of the body instead of healing it with nutrition, give radiation or chemotherapy, which are all unnatural to the body and can often make the situation worse.

I always thought that if the human body were originally meant to be opened up, it would have a zip on it. But health problems are often left to the last minute, which can often result in emergency procedures. In most cancer cases, the radiation and chemo kills the patient even before the actual disease does because it not only kills the bad cells but the good ones also and leaves the body with a toxic overload whilst breaking down the immune system, making the body ineffective of healing itself.

Only the correct fuel that was created for the proper functioning of the body and building of the cells and organs can reverse the process, allowing the body to heal itself naturally as it was designed to do. Nobody can change or beat nature, no matter the man-made technology, life is much simpler when we observe the natural laws of nature.

To help guide you as to what herbs can be helpful to you, I have compiled a list of some favourite well-known herbs and seeds. I have also included some nutritional values and ailments they have been known to help. There are thousands more herbs out there, even in our gardens that could be healing us.

There is various information in books and on the Internet that shows you how to identify these herbs and what your body can use them to cure. Always seek the advice of a herbalist or naturopath if you have not used herbs before or learn how to use them for yourself.

Moringa Oleifera

The most remarkable tree and herb I have come across. It's a food that comes in many varieties; it is found mainly in Africa, India and different parts of the world. Moringa is known in certain countries as the miracle tree because of its remarkable near-perfect contents of almost all the of vitamins, minerals and amino acids the body needs; it contains over 40 amino acids and all nine of the essential amino acids the body requires.

Moringa contains chlorophyll, A, C, B vitamins, calcium, potassium and other vitamins, minerals and protein. Every part of the tree can be used. It has been used to prevent malnutrition. The most remarkable thing is that the areas of the world that you find the highest incidents of malnutrition are the same areas that the tree grows. Many people around the world have recovered from all sorts of diseases and ailments after taking Moringa. The list of ailments would be too long to include here. You can also add it to your food and juices. The seeds are used to filter water. There are many products such as tea, soaps, creams, oils, etc. made from Moringa.

It also contains arginine, an amino acid that helps keep your blood vessels open, smooth and healthy, and helps with your circulation and supports bone health, as well as many other benefits and helping to balance the alkaline acid environment of the body.

Alfalfa Sprouts

Has been used as a remedy in China, India and Europe. Alfalfa contains chlorophyll, protein, minerals, beta-carotene, B vitamins, and vitamins C, E, and K. Alfalfa has been used for indigestion, arthritis, bladder problems, high cholesterol, hay fever, and irregular menstruation.

Being in its chlorophyll content makes it great for the alkaline balance of the blood.

Alfalfa is best known as a food that is used in salads and sandwiches. The raw sprouts can be found in grocery and health food shops. Sprouted seed is also known as a living food, meaning it still contains all the enzymes and nutrients needed for the body to be nourished.

Basil Leaves

Basil leaves are naturally full of aroma and add a slight sweet flavour to food. It is used in all types of dishes. Its antispasmodic properties mean that it can be used as a medicine for nausea and motion sickness but at the same time because of its strong taste and smell can be quite nauseating for some people. You either love it or hate it.

Basil contains folic acid, potassium, iron and calcium. It provides fibre and protein as well as Vitamins A, B, C, E, iron, magnesium, selenium, manganese, copper, phosphorous, potassium and zinc. Basil also has anti-bacterial properties.

Cinnamon

Like most natural herbs and spices, cinnamon has been around since ancient times. The bark of the cinnamon tree is dried and rolled into cinnamon sticks or dried and ground into a powder. Cinnamon has extremely high anti-oxidant levels; the oil it produces has strong anti-bacterial and anti-fungal properties. It is also a great source of manganese, fibre, iron, and calcium. As a result, it has been used as an effective home remedy for reducing blood sugar levels, treating Diabetes, lowering bad cholesterol, aiding digestion, treating diarrhoea, curing the common cold, reduces arthritis pain, boosting memory and cognitive function, treating toothaches, eliminating bad breath, curing headaches and migraine pain and so many other conditions.

Dandelion

Dandelion leaves are very nutritious and contain beta-carotene, which is very good for the eyes, skin, and hair. They are also a good source of vitamins B1, B2, B5, B6, B12, C, and E. It is used as a remedy for liver complaints as well as many other ailments such as inflammation, skin conditions and kidney problems such as jaundice and cirrhosis of the liver. The roots were traditionally brewed into beverages. I remember as a child that dandelion and burdock cordial was quite popular in the UK.
Dandelion root coffee is delicious with a bit of added coconut or almond milk and a healthy natural sweetener.

Echinacea

Echinacea is known as an immune system booster. It's used for colds, flu, and other infections in order to boost the immune system to fight off the infection.

Because it strengthens the immune system, it will begin its work in curing all sorts of ailments as well as being applied topically to speed up cuts and bruises. Echinacea is also used for gum disease and urinary tract and other infections.

Ginger

Ginger is a root used in cooking as well as medicinally. It's great in ginger beer and adding to smoothies.

Ginger has been known to be beneficial for conditions caused by lack of blood circulation such as angina, clotting, menstruation problems, preventing blood platelets from sticking together as well as other ailments such as lowering bad cholesterol, sore throat, colds, coughs, bronchitis, arthritis and stomach problems such as gas, cramps, diarrhoea, nausea, motion sickness, and ginger tea is also popular for eliminating morning sickness.

Blended ginger and garlic in hot water, strained to remove the stringy bits, with added lemon and honey is very good for colds and flu.

Garlic

Garlic, a family of the onion that has many medicinal uses as well as cooking, of course, has been used around the world even dating back to the ancients.

Garlic has antibacterial properties and is a great natural antibiotic. I discovered that one clove of garlic is stronger than many antibiotic tablets, but without the side effects. Garlic is also good for cleaning the blood, promoting good blood circulation and acts as a natural blood thinner.

Garlic can fight arterial plaque, improve the elasticity of arteries, and reduce blood clotting and can lower bad cholesterol and high blood pressure.

Garlic is loaded with minerals such as Manganese, copper, iron, zinc, sulfur, calcium and selenium. There is a bit of controversy around garlic, but so far I have noticed only health benefits that is why I have included it here, but again do your own research and go with your own body's response.

Hemp seeds
Hemp seeds and hemp oil have a very high nutritional value as well as the seed being very fibrous and contain a variety of vitamins and minerals, they are an essential fatty acid (EFA) they contain protein as well as all the amino acids, Making hemp milk is very quick and easy. They can also be sprinkled on salads. Have a look at the recipes section at the end of the book for hemp milk. Hemp oil is great for drizzling on salads or adding to smoothies an easy way of getting your daily dose of EFA's
Hemp is also a very versatile material that can be use industrially to make paper, clothes, shoes and bags etc.

Nettle
The stinging nettle as it's also known, was not a favourite of mine when I was young, as I was always getting stung by running though bushes, then I would have to find a doc leaf to calm the stinging. It is excellent though for making very tasty non-alcoholic beers teas, and wines, it has great health benefits such as relief of PMS, arthritis, kidney stones, asthma, hay fever, bladder infection anaemia and Alzheimer's among many other benefits.
Nettle has a very high content of iron, so very good for all forms of anaemia. It helps to remove uric acid from the joints so very good for gout sufferers. It also contains other minerals such as calcium, potassium, magnesium, manganese and sodium among others and a good source of Vitamin C and B complex.

Turmeric
A warm spice loaded with health benefits and used extensively in Indian cooking, as a colouring agent and as a food preservative worldwide in foods such as mustard, pickles, cheeses and margarine.

Turmeric has recently hit the headlines because of claims that curcumin, the main active constituent of turmeric, could help prevent dementia and Alzheimer's disease as well as heart disease and boosting energy levels. Also a natural anti-inflammatory, which can work as an alternative to pharmaceutical anti-inflammatory without the side effects.

Turmeric is high in iron, zinc, manganese, as well as potassium, Vitamin C, E, B6 and niacin.

FRUITS

FRUITS HAVE MORE BENEFITS WHEN EATEN ON AN EMPTY STOMACH.

Dr Stephen Mak treats terminal ill cancer patients by an "unorthodox" way and many patients recovered. Before he used solar energy to clear the illnesses of his patients, he believes that fruits and juicing are one of the strategies in healing cancer and contributed to the article below.

When you eat fruit on an empty stomach or before, rather than after your meals, it plays a major role to detoxify your system. It can supply you with a great deal of energy and weight loss. This applies to salads also.

If you eat a piece of bread and then some fruit, the fruit is ready to go straight through the stomach into the intestines, but it is prevented from doing so by the bread.
In the meantime, everything you have just eaten, ferments, rots and turns acidic, leaving an overload of acid in your system. The minute the fruit comes into contact with the food in the stomach and digestive juices, the entire mass of food begins to spoil.
The fruit mixes with the putrefying other food and produces gas and causes you to bloat.
So it is much easier on your system when you eat your fruits on an empty stomach or before your main meals rather than after.

Many people believe that oranges and lemons are acidic, this may be true, but all fruits become alkaline in our body, according to Dr. H. Shelton, who did research on this matter. If you have mastered the correct way of eating fruits, you have another secret of beauty, longevity, health, energy, and normal weight.
When you need to drink fruit juice — drink only fresh fruit juice,

NOT from concentrate or the cans ... Fruit juice can be very sweet so you may need to water it down a bit. Don't drink juice that has been heated up. Don't eat cooked fruits because you don't get the nutrients at all. You only get the taste. Cooking fruit destroys all the enzymes and vitamins.

Eating a whole fruit is better than drinking the juice because you get the fibre also. But if you need a boost of energy, then drinking the juice will go straight to the blood and give you steady energy levels. If you drink the juice, drink it mouthful by mouthful slowly because you must let it mix with your saliva before swallowing, this helps it to assimilate into your system.

If you have quite a clean system from regular cleanses and eating the correct food, you can go on a three-day fruit fast to cleanse your body without doing a deep cleanse with capsules, etc. Just eat fruits and drink fruit juice and good water throughout the three days, and you will be surprised how you feel and look. You may want to start more slowly, and transition into it if this is your first time doing a cleanse. But use natural organic fruits. Look out for hybrid, GMO and seedless fruits as they are very sweet and contain unhealthy starch and can cause health problems.

KIWI: Tiny but mighty. This is a good source of potassium, magnesium, vitamin E & fibre. Its vitamin C content is twice that of an orange.

APPLE: Although an apple has low vitamin C content, it has antioxidants & flavonoids, which enhances the activity of vitamin C thereby helping to lower the risks of colon cancer, heart attack & stroke.

STRAWBERRY: Protective Fruit. Strawberries have one of the highest total antioxidant power among major fruits & protect the body from cancer-causing, blood vessel-clogging free radicals that destroy the cells and age the skin.

If you are blessed enough to live somewhere where coconuts grow in abundance, you should take the opportunity to have at least one a day. When I'm in Ghana, I have two or three coconuts a day. The first time I took my husband to Ghana, he got all of the recommended vaccine shots and was terribly ill from them; the second time and every time after that, he did not go for any shots, we just had our one or two coconuts a day, and for the whole year that we were there, he or I had no problems whatsoever with malaria despite having mosquito bites; to tell the truth, we use to get just as many bites from mosquitos in Holland, UK and Spain where we have lived. Read some more incredible benefits below of coconuts, courtesy of the coconut research center.org

The coconut provides a nutritious source of meat, juice, milk, and oil that has fed and nourished populations around the world for generations. On many islands, coconut is a staple in the diet and provides the majority of the food eaten. Nearly one-third of the world's population depends on coconut to some degree for their food and their economy. Among these cultures, the coconut has a long and respected history.

Coconut is highly nutritious and rich in fibre, vitamins, and minerals. It is classified as a "functional food" because it provides many health benefits beyond its nutritional content. Coconut oil is of special interest because it possesses healing properties far beyond that of any other dietary oil and is extensively used in traditional medicine among Asian and Pacific populations. Pacific Islanders consider coconut oil to be the cure for all illness. The coconut palm is so highly valued by them as both a source of food and medicine that it is called "The Tree of Life." Only recently has modern medical science unlocked the secrets to coconut's amazing healing powers.

Coconut In Traditional Medicine

People from many diverse cultures, languages, religions, and races scattered around the globe have revered the coconut as a valuable source of both food and medicine. Wherever the coconut palm grows, the people have learned of its importance as an effective medicine. For thousands of years, coconut products have held a respected and valuable place in local folk medicine.

In traditional medicine around the world, coconut is used to treat a wide variety of health problems including the following: abscesses, asthma, baldness, bronchitis, bruises, burns, colds, constipation, cough, dropsy, dysentery, earache, fever, flu, gingivitis, gonorrhoea, irregular or painful menstruation, jaundice, kidney stones, lice, malnutrition, nausea, rash, scabies, scurvy, skin infections, sore throat, swelling, syphilis, toothache, tuberculosis, tumours, typhoid, ulcers, upset stomach, weakness, and wounds.

Coconut In Modern Medicine

Modern medical science is now confirming the use of coconut in treating many of the above conditions. Published studies in medical journals show that coconut, in one form or another, may provide a wide range of health benefits. Some of these are summarised below:

- Kills viruses that cause influenza, herpes, measles, hepatitis C, SARS, AIDS, and other illnesses.
- Kills bacteria that cause ulcers, throat infections, urinary tract infections, gum disease and cavities, pneumonia, and gonorrhoea, and other diseases.
- Kills fungi and yeasts that cause candidiasis, ringworm, athlete's foot, thrush, diaper rash, and other infections.

- Expels or kills tapeworms, lice, giardia, and other parasites.
- Provides a nutritional source of quick energy.
- Boosts energy and endurance, enhancing physical and athletic performance.
- Improves digestion and absorption of other nutrients including vitamins, minerals, and amino acids.
- Improves insulin secretion and utilisation of blood glucose.
- Relieves stress on pancreas and enzyme systems of the body.
- Reduces symptoms associated with pancreatitis.
- Helps relieve symptoms and reduces health risks associated with diabetes.
- Reduces problems associated with malabsorption syndrome and cystic fibrosis.
- Improves calcium and magnesium absorption and supports the development of strong bones and teeth.
- Helps protect against osteoporosis.
- Helps relieve symptoms associated with gallbladder disease.
- Relieves symptoms associated with Crohn's disease, ulcerative colitis, and stomach ulcers.
- Improves digestion and bowel function.
- Relieves pain and irritation caused by haemorrhoids.
- Reduces inflammation.
- Supports tissue healing and repair.
- Supports and aids immune system function.
- Helps protect the body from breast, colon and other cancers.
- Is heart healthy; improves cholesterol ratio reducing risk of heart disease.
- Protects arteries from injury that causes atherosclerosis and thus protects against heart disease.
- Helps prevent periodontal disease and tooth decay.

- Functions as a protective antioxidant.
- Helps to protect the body from harmful free radicals that promote premature ageing and degenerative disease.
- Does not deplete the body's antioxidant reserves like other oils do.
- Improves utilisation of essential fatty acids and protects them from oxidation.
- Helps relieve symptoms associated with chronic fatigue syndrome.
- Relieves symptoms associated with benign prostatic hyperplasia (prostate enlargement).
- Reduces epileptic seizures.
- Helps protect against kidney disease and bladder infections.
- Dissolves kidney stones.
- Helps prevent liver disease.
- Is lower in calories than all other fats.
- Supports thyroid function.
- Promotes loss of excess weight by increasing metabolic rate.
- Is utilised by the body to produce energy in preference to being stored as body fat like other dietary fats.
- Helps prevent obesity and overweight problems.
- Applied topically helps to form a chemical barrier on the skin to ward off infection.
- Reduces symptoms associated with psoriasis, eczema, and dermatitis.
- Supports the natural chemical balance of the skin.
- Softens skin and helps relieve dryness and flaking.
- Prevents wrinkles, sagging skin, and age spots.
- Promotes healthy looking hair and complexion.
- Provides protection from damaging effects of ultraviolet radiation from the sun.
- Helps control dandruff.

My recent research confirmed that sunlight alone does not cause skin cancer, as the sunscreen companies, dermatologist and the multi-million-cancer industry, have told us. In fact, sunlight actually prevents skin cancer, bone cancer and other types of cancers. Research has also revealed that melanoma is more common in people that stay out of the sun more than people that are constantly in the sun; you don't have to over-do it, but we all need sunshine and vitamin D.

It has been found that it's not sunlight alone that causes skin cancer, but a reaction between sunlight and the condition of your skin. Sunlight, plus nutritional deficiency and a high-fat diet (bad fats) can cause sunburn, leading to skin cancer.

Good nutrition builds our immune system as well as provides protection for our internal organs and our skin. When we increase our nutritional intake, especially antioxidants that fight free radicals and minimise oxidation, it allows our skin cells to rebuild itself properly and so protects the skin, making it more resistant and preventing sunburn that can lead to skin cancer.

The body needs vitamin D, and vitamin D is better obtained naturally from the sun, although you can get sources of vitamin D supplements, especially if you live in a country that has minimum sunshine in the winter months. A lack of Vitamin D, C and a low immune system will always cause you to have colds in the winter months. If you build up your immune system by eating a good natural plant-based diet and supplementing as well as getting enough vitamin D, you can minimise your risk of getting that seasonal flu that always goes around.

When skin is exposed to the sun, it manufactures vitamin D. If you do not get enough sunlight, you will be deficient in vitamin D. Recent studies showed that Vitamin D prevents many different types of cancers, so if you are not getting enough, you may be at a risk.

The darker your skin, the more melanin you have. Melanin is an amazing substance that gives skin and hair its colour. I have been researching Melanin recently and found that it is responsible for far more than our skin colour. It's also called pigment. Melanin also acts as a barrier and limits the amount of Vitamin D that you get through the skin, so if you have darker skin, you need much more sun exposure to get a sufficient amount of vitamin D on your skin.

Everybody has Melanin, but the lighter your skin, the less Melanin you have, if your skin is very light, you still have Melanin but not as much, so you will need less sun exposure for the skin to manufacture vitamin D. So the answer is not to put lots of sunscreen on your body as some of the ingredients in sunscreen have been reported to actually cause cancer, as they contain cancer causing substances and various toxins.

The answer is to make sure you have a good nutritional intake to build up your immune system, have very high antioxidant levels from foods such as berries, green leafy vegetables combined with sunshine. This can prevent sunburn, skin cancer and other types of cancers. If you need sunscreen because of sensitive skin, try to find one that is natural and does not contain cancer-causing toxins. Coconut oil applied before you get into the sun can give protection against sunburn. For sunburn, aloe vera gel is great for soothing and healing sunburn.

Other Benefits of Sunlight
Sunlight enhances the immune system function in the following ways:
1. Increases lymphocyte numbers and stimulates B- and T-cell functions.
2. Lowers blood cholesterol
3. Increases tolerance to stress
The ultraviolet rays not only kill microbes invading the skin but fight internal infections also. Sunlight promotes elimination of pollutants such as toxic metals from the body through your sweat and helps the body to cope with physical stress imposed by exposure to pollutants.

Melatonin
When light enters the eyes, it affects the pineal gland in the brain, which affects melatonin. Melatonin is a hormone produced by the pineal gland, and some of its influences are:
1. Hormone production of the pituitary, adrenals, thyroid and sex organs.
2. Relaxation
3. Sleep induction
4. Mood/behaviour
5. The body's defences against cancer

Produced during the dark hours, melatonin secretion is inhibited by bright light. The light-dark cycle synchronises the body's biological clock. Disturbances of our time clock disrupt melatonin production. Low levels of melatonin are seen with stress and psychological disorders, such as depression, anxiety attacks and bipolar disorder.

Studies have shown that bright, early morning light exposure improves depression.   The bright, morning light gives an antidepressant effect on the mind and body.

Along with clean water and fresh air — sunshine has healing and life-giving powers, so we do not have to hide ourselves from the sun but rather come to the knowledge of its healing benefits. Especially if you are sick, you will gain a great deal in your health by being in the sunshine and being in an atmosphere where you can breathe in deep fresh air.

CHAPTER 10

Hereditary Conditions?

I believe that the common chronic conditions of today, linked to our diet and lifestyle are not hereditary, and most can be reversed. Modern diseases are a result of our modern toxins environment and the toxins we consume.
The common chronic conditions of today are not hereditary, as we may have been told. They are lifestyle diseases of the body. I have heard so many times that chronic conditions such as cancer, heart disease, stroke, diabetes, and asthma, etc. are hereditary. It may be true that your grandmother had diabetes for example, and your mother has diabetes and now you have diabetes. However, does that mean that it's hereditary, or could it be the diet that is hereditary causing the same conditions?

You will shortly see that diabetes is simply an overload of sugar and bad fats in the blood, mainly artificial sugars as well as bad carbohydrates in processed foods that convert to sugar once it enters the body.

So if your grandmother had a diet of high sugar, processed foods or some of the dangerous foods we mentioned, your mother would most probably have been raised on the same diet and you also would probably eat the same foods that you ate at home, unless you become aware.

So does it not make more sense that as chronic diseases have not always existed, that it's more likely linked to what we eat, and it's rather the diet that is hereditary rather than the condition? I'm just trying to get people to use common sense and to think outside of the box, but we know this to be true because when people with diabetes cleanse the excess sugar and bad fats from their blood and give the body what it needs, everything goes back to normal, and there is no more diabetes. I have seen this so many times.

However, there are some hereditary conditions but not the common chronic conditions of today. So if you do have diabetes, make sure you do something about it before it deteriorates and you end up having unnecessary operations, or even bits cut from your body when it could have been reversed.

So if you change your diet to a more nutritious living diet and you give the same nutritious foods to your children, you can be sure that as long as your children continue to eat the same nutritious foods they ate at home, they too will not have any problems with diabetes. The same is true for heart disease and other so-called hereditary conditions, especially the common chronic conditions of today linked to the standard tradition diet. It's all about prevention.

Women have to be careful about what they eat before as well as when they are pregnant, as everything you eat and drink, the baby eats and drinks the same thing and this can be harmful to the baby when they are in the womb right through to when they are born. Through what you eat, you could be setting your baby up for a chronic condition before they are born, and you don't even know it.

This is why I believe that some babies are born with certain conditions that could have been prevented if only the mothers were given the correct information. I also believe that pregnant women should not drink alcohol at all.

When you drink alcohol, it goes into your system and bloodstream just like anything else you eat and drink; as the baby is fed and watered through what you eat and drink, it is quite obvious that if you drink alcohol when pregnant it will also go through to the baby just like the food and other liquids you may drink. There is now proof of this with alcohol foetal syndrome.

In the medical field, if they find you have a family history of a condition that may leave you susceptible to it, in cases such as breast cancer or ovarian cancer, etc. if they think you may get any of these conditions in future, they will not teach you how to prevent it through nutrition and cleansing. They may just suggest having that part of the body removed, just in case. It sounds absurd, but people are actually having body parts removed for prevention while there is a much easier way of prevention.

Life is only complicated when we complicate it. The biggest problem we have with illness and so-called disease is LACK of KNOWLEDGE or IGNORANCE. As well as giving all responsibility for our health and families' health to someone else. At the end of the day, we only know what we know and what we don't know could be harming or even killing us.

Diabetes - The Real Truth

What is Diabetes?

And why is it circulating to almost epidemic proportions around the world? After years of reviewing, researching and taking a look at so-called diabetes; one of my teachers and mentors, Dr J Johnson came to a conclusion that there is no such thing as type 2 diabetes, only high sugar levels. And excess fat in the blood.

The question was asked, what is so-called type 2 diabetes? The definition was that it was a disease that is caused by high sugar levels in the blood. New evidence has shown that you don't have to have high blood pressure or high sugar levels and that diabetes is not a hereditary trait; they are both caused by the same thing, dirty, sticky blood. By cleansing the blood, you will lower cholesterol, sugar levels and blood pressure. Additionally, you'll get good circulation going in the body again.

So back to the definition of diabetes — it's a disease caused by high sugar levels in the blood. So the next question is:

How did the sugar get into the blood?

Many people with diabetes check their sugar levels on a daily basis by pricking the end of their finger to extract and test a little bit of blood. Also, remember that if you continue to prick your finger, it will become numb, and you can kill the nerve endings in that finger. So by pricking the finger, you are able to test the amount of sugar in your blood, the results will tell you how high your sugar level is or how much sugar is in your blood.

The question asked: How did the sugar get in your blood? And the answer is that you put it there. There is no other way for the sugar to get in the blood unless you put it there. So if that is true, then how did you put it there? By what you eat and what you drink on a daily basis. It's that simple. That is the only way that the sugar can get in your blood. Now if this is true, what foods and drinks are causing this?

Just before we move to the foods, it is important to note that if a pregnant woman has high sugar levels in her blood because she is feeding her unborn child with the same foods that she eats, it's possible that the baby could also have high sugar levels when they are born leading to type 1 childhood diabetes.

As we saw before, it is the same dangerous foods most people eat daily — these are the same dead foods we saw earlier that contribute to diabetes and other chronic conditions.

White sugar — including sugar substitutes, white flour — (white flour is especially dangerous) this includes anything that is made with white processed flour or meals: cakes, pies, cookies, donuts, pizzas and white pasta, etc., soft drinks, red meat, coffee, tea, punch, (juices from concentrates from the grocery stores). Pasteurised dairy products, i.e. all pasteurised animal milk and products such as cheese and cream.
Animal fats, i.e. pasteurised butter, lard, margarine, bacon grease, corn oil and other saturated fats. Also, if you have high sugar levels, stay away from hybrid banana, grapes, orange and orange juice, these are all without seeds, as they contain far more sugar and can raise your sugar levels immediately.

So who controls your sugar levels?
The answer is simple: You do! Suppose I were to eat a big cake, then wash it down with a large glass of juice or a sugary drink, my sugar levels would be about 300, at that particular time if I went to the doctor, I would probably be labelled as diabetic and put on insulin and sugar pills, but does that mean I am really diabetic or

does it mean that I have been given the wrong information by being indoctrinated to believe I am 'so-called diabetic.'

The truth is that I just dump all of this sugar in my blood, and that is what is causing the high sugar levels. I'm not diabetic; I'm simply putting lots of sugar in my blood.
Here's what the average person does every day. When they get up, they have a cup of coffee. The coffee already contains sugar, and they put two spoons of sugar in it, and then they will have a large bowl of cereal. Cereal is sugar to the body, then they will put more sugar in it, then maybe some banana and some raisins, more sugar, then they will have a piece of toast, which is also sugar to the body. Next, they will probably put some jam on top of it, yet more sugar, then they will wash it down with a large glass of orange juice. Their sugar level by now is probably between 300-500. Are they diabetic or have they just sugar loaded?

So you see how there is no such thing as type 2 diabetes. People are just sugar loading on a daily basis and ending up with high sugar levels and being put on insulin and sugar pills and other types of pills for the rest of their lives. What a big shame.

Do insulin and sugar pills take the sugar out of the blood?
The answer is no; this is the reason you are told to stay on them for the rest of your life. So if they do not take the sugar out of the blood, why are people still taking it? Because this is all they know, and that's what they've been told to do, it's just a lack of knowledge on both parts.

Did you know that the pancreas, which secretes insulin, only burns up natural sugar? So all of that artificial sugar goes straight to the blood, when that happens you are considered a diabetic, but are you really diabetic?

160

As a result of the artificial sugars raising your sugar levels, your sugar levels will always be high, and the doctor will tell you to stay on the medication for the rest of your life rather than getting the artificial sugar out of your blood and keeping it out by not consuming the foods and drinks that cause this.

A friend of mine mentioned that he had been diagnosed as diabetic and very high blood pressure; I recommended he cut out the foods on the dangerous foods list, which he managed to do and started to eat cleansing foods such as more fruits and vegetables. He tested himself a few weeks later and noticed that his blood sugar had dropped to normal. He went to the doctor and told her, she said that it was impossible; he said I beg to differ. So she tested him and confirmed that his blood sugar had indeed dropped to normal, and his high blood pressure was normal also. It's not rocket science; it's common sense.

My in-laws came to visit us; while they were with us, of course, we only gave them healthy foods. They both had so-called diabetes when they arrived, but when they got back home, they went to their doctor's appointment, and the doctor was surprised that neither of them had diabetes anymore.

Two weeks before they came to visit, she had a heart attack, they thought they would have to postpone the trip, but the doctor gave her a last minute go ahead to be able to travel. When they got back home, the doctor examined her and was shocked because her heart was much stronger than the last time she was examined. The doctor was so impressed with all of this that he had made copies of the common foods list they gave him and started distributing it to his customers. That is the kind of doctor that cares, and the type of doctor I like, because if all of his patients got well, it would affect his business but has still chosen to hand out the list to help his patients. What a great doctor.

What is the solution for too much sugar in the blood?
The only way to get the sugar out of the blood is to keep it out and clean it out, and you can do that with internal cleansing or cleansing living raw foods. You can also research and find a good natural blood cleanser. There is scientific proof that we must cleanse our blood on a regular basis to avoid heart attack and strokes.

There is no doubt that "Life is in the blood" and as we eat and drink dead processed foods we clog up the blood, making it thick and dirty. Clots can form and cause heart attacks, strokes and poor circulation through the body. If you have numbness in the little finger or dull pain in your shoulder or arm or pain in your chest whenever you walk up a flight of stairs, you may be in stroke territory right now!

There are many natural products as well as cleansing foods as mentioned before, such as arginine, ginger, parsley, garlic, lemon, green leafy vegetables, basil, wheatgrass juice and beetroot that can do an excellent job of cleaning and building the blood.

Sickle Cell Anaemia

Very little has been written on sickle cell anaemia also known as sickle cell disease in the last ten years. Conventional medicine seems to have come to a halt as far as treatment is concerned. There is no drug that we know of that can help a person with sickle cell anaemia. Maybe that's because drugs are not the answer, but nutrition as I discovered for myself.

The problems associated with sickle-shaped blood cells damaged and clogged blood vessels and subsequent tissue and organ damage, can be prevented and minimised with certain foods and nutrients. Don't worry about all the talk about genes. Blaming genetics leaves us with the impression that nothing can be done about it. The important thing is to concentrate on what happens and what can be done to alleviate the effects.

Sickle cell primarily affects those of African and West Indian descendants, but it also occurs in some individuals of Mediterranean, Middle Eastern, and Asian Indian descent. To simplify matters, doctors explain it as a genetic defect causing distortion of haemoglobin (red blood) cells into sickle shapes, slowing, or even stopping the flow of blood and decreasing the amount of oxygen the red blood cells are able to carry.

The result is basically a loss of circulating oxygen and blood to body tissues and organs. The excruciating pain and constant infections and organ damage is a result of this loss of circulation and oxygen. Sickle cell patients are told that there is no cure for this inherited defect. Studies have shown that increasing the oxygen levels in the blood of arteries temporarily restores the haemoglobin to normal and oxygenating and can prevent, at least temporarily, the blood cells from deforming.

There are nutrients that increase blood oxygen and circulation that have been shown to help the sickle cell syndrome. One of the early symptoms of circulation blockages is joint pain, and muscle cramping that is caused by inadequate oxygen and red blood cells clumping together, which is what happens when red blood cells deform and sickle. So the answer would be separating those cells. Another one of my mentors Dr Sebi, discovered that in Sickle cell sufferers, the blood cells are covered with mucus, hence the deformation of the cell and oxygen not being able to get to the cells. This makes sense. So it's possible that the cleansing I have been doing has also been cleansing mucus from my cells, and this along with a high intake of nutrition is the reason I no longer have symptoms.

These are some recommendations by Doctor. Johnson. If you have sickle cell, you should begin to use herbal products that can cleanse the blood on a regular basis. Cleansing the blood is the most important thing that a person with sickle cell can do. I used herbal products that helped to build my blood — making red blood cells is the second most important thing that a person with sickle cell can do. Making blood is like making a cake; you must have all the right kinds of ingredients.

What you need:
Vitamin C an antioxidant, essential also for maintaining smooth, flexible arterial walls necessary for proper blood circulation. Vitamin B complex (never take any one B vitamin by itself — this can cause the other B's to be depleted from the body. Therefore, never just take folic acid, always get a B-complex with all the B vitamins and make sure that all of the B's are the same milligrams; except the folic acid, which should be 400 mcg. B Vitamins promote healthier and more numerous red blood cells.

Natural Iron. Eating a diet rich in iron can help your haemoglobin level stay high enough so that all the cells in your body get the oxygen they need to function properly and efficiently.

Zinc has been shown to reduce the amount of irreversible sickle cells and increase the longevity of red blood cells.

Vitamin E breaks up clumping and increases oxygen to the cells. Help your body make blood by taking yellow dock root and bugleweed herb.

Help your body to make Vitamin D on the skin from the sun. Take plant-based minerals on a daily basis.

Change your diet drastically and eat the right foods, a good percentage of raw living foods to feed your cells.

Moringa Oleifera as seen before contains virtually all essential vitamins, minerals and amino acids and taken on a daily basis will be extremely beneficial for getting circulation going, feeding the cells and getting oxygen into the blood and so reducing pain. My brother uses Moringa whenever he gets a sickle cell crisis coming on, and he says this stops the crisis within a short time. Your diet should also consist of the blood cleansing and blood building foods and herbs we mentioned earlier, such as arginine, ginger, parsley, garlic, lemon, green leafy vegetables, basil, wheatgrass juice and beetroot. To maintain oxygen levels in my blood and cells, as well as doing all the above, I also take activated stabilised oxygen drops.

Note: You can live a better and longer life without any crisis and hospital visits when you begin to live this way. I am living testimony and proof of this.

Some Statistics of Chronic Conditions

As we all know by now, chronic diseases are increasing at an alarming rate every year. I have added this information to show you exactly how much chronic conditions are increasing with the hope that people will be motivated to do something about prevention today! And not leave their health to chance.

Chronic diseases are diseases of long duration and generally slow progression. Chronic diseases, such as heart disease, stroke, cancer, chronic respiratory diseases and diabetes, are by far the leading cause of mortality in the world, representing 60% of all deaths. Out of the 35 million people who died from chronic disease in 2005, half were under 70, and half were women.

Current statistics show that 90% of people will die prematurely as a result of their diet. This is shocking statistics, but the fact is that it is actually happening in reality.

Asthma is a chronic disease of the bronchial, the air passages leading to and from the lungs. Some 300 million people currently suffer from asthma. It is the most common chronic disease among children.

Cancer is a leading cause of death worldwide: it accounted for 7.4 million deaths (around 13% of all deaths) in 2004.

Lung, stomach, liver, colon and breast cancer cause the most cancer deaths each year. Over one million new colon cancer patients diagnosed each year. More than 600,000 colon cancer-related mortalities occur annually.

Cardiovascular disease - CVDs are the number one cause of death globally: more people die annually from CVDs than from any other cause.

really does pay to do your own research. As we mentioned before, increasing environmental pollution is contributing in weakening the immune system, which will result in increased susceptibility to disease.

The current lead content of human bones has been found to be 1400 times greater than the lead levels in bones from an ancient civilisation. In children, low dose lead exposure has significant long-term effects on many central nervous system functions such as lower IQ scores and poorer hand-eye coordination. We also mentioned that stress suppresses the immune system. Other factors that cause greater damage to the immune system are psychological stresses, loss of a job or serious illness in oneself or a family member, which can also lead to depression. One of the most stressful events, the death of a partner or a close family member, has been associated with immune system suppression and increased mortality in the grieving partner.
Boost your immune system by controlling stress levels and eating a balanced plant-based diet regularly.

Malnutrition
Malnutrition does not just happen amongst the starving people around the world as we think.

You can be malnourished by not getting the nutrition the body needs to function correctly. When you look at western malnutrition and the diseases, it's an epidemic. People are getting more obese but yet extremely malnourished and literally eating themselves to death with lifeless foods.

Being under-nourished, or deficiency is the most frequent cause of impaired immunity. Deficiencies of essential minerals and nutrients can result in poor immune system performance and overall health.

Drugs, radiation, chemotherapy, laser treatment and surgical operations are known to suppress immune functions. In addition, radiation and anti-cancer drugs have serious long-term complications.

Drugs such as aspirin, antihistamines, nasal decongestant, adrenal hormone preparations (cortisol creams) and unnatural female hormone preparations (Progesterone and Oestrogen) all suppress or impair the immune response. If you use a progesterone cream for certain female hormonal conditions, it will be more beneficial to look at balancing your hormones through a plant-based diet and include good fats, or looking for a natural progesterone cream without the chemicals. There are plenty on the market nowadays. Just research and find the correct one for you.

Proper care of the immune system can safeguard against immune disease. The best way to strengthen or restore your immune system again is to simply live a balanced natural living food diet and lifestyle.

Rest and Sleep
One of the most underestimated immune stimulators is proper rest and sleep. The body requires both phases of sleep, rapid eye movement (REM) sleep and non-rapid eye movement (NREM) sleep.

REM sleep deprivation causes irritability and significant psychological changes. Both emotional states have detrimental effects on immune functions. Non-REM sleep is essential for the immune system's peak performance in sweeping out foreign invaders. Individuals deprived of NREM sleep become sluggish, depressed, and find it hard to focus or concentrate.

NREM sleep is also a great anti-ageing tool. Making sure that you get enough sleep will keep you younger looking, especially when you sleep earlier rather than late as this is when your cells are renewed and repaired, between the hours of 10 and 11 at night. We are all different and need different sleep requirements. I need at least seven-eight hours sleep, but some can manage on only five hours sleep, but the benefits come from sleeping early.

During the NREM hours, growth hormones, secreted by the pituitary glands, aids in repair or replacement of the bone and other body cells, including those of the immune system.

Some people suffer from insomnia, a more serious condition of sleep deprivation. Sometimes this can be caused by worry and stress, try to empty your mind before you sleep and try the deep breath exercises mentioned earlier.

The Colon

One of the body's primary organs of elimination is the colon. It can hold several pounds of backed-up waste, drug residue, putrefied food, pesticides, parasites and worms. Yuck! (Even more so when you eat meat that is not properly cooked or raw fish and other damaging chemicals making the body toxic, leading to toxic-related illnesses)

All of these substances have to be removed from the body; otherwise, it will lead to other serious health issues. I mentioned earlier that health begins in the gut. Cleansing the colon can clear the pathway for other toxins to leave the body. The colon needs to be regulated so that you are moving your bowels twice a day if you eat twice a day and to remove any toxins and excess mucus.

Because of lifeless foods, our body has a hard time dealing with this, and our liver and organs struggle to function properly. Our digestive system cannot cope, so it does not effectively digest most of these foods, leaving them to accumulate in our system and the body cannot eliminate the waste within the time frame of 30-60 minutes after you have eaten.

Remember that a clean colon is fundamental to good health. It's also the first step to good health.

The Liver

The most important organ in your body for getting rid of toxic build up and Xenoestrogens (man-made synthetic chemicals) in the liver. The second largest organ performing over 200 tasks, it assists digestion, manages fat storage, neutralises toxins, metabolises drugs, supports the immune system, kills bacteria and maintains hormone balance. The liver maintains a balance of hormones by secreting enzymes, chemical messengers that break down the molecular structure of the hormone through a series of chemical reactions. It then converts them to inactive compounds that can be safely removed from the body through the urine. Effective functioning of the liver can be damaged by eating the wrong diet, alcohol consumption, lack of exercise, taking prescription drugs or recreational drugs, exposure to heavy metals, toxins and Xenoestrogens.

The chemicals overload the liver, forcing it to work harder, and diverting energy from the liver's regular activities such as recycling oestrogen and maintaining a healthy balance with fat stores. When the liver is busy trying to filter all the toxins that come into the body from the wrong foods, it cannot adequately burn the fat as it's meant to do. This can lead to consequences such as obesity and problems in general with losing weight, low energy levels, digestive problems, infertility, endometriosis and increased fibroid growth.

You can keep your liver healthy by cleansing the liver. This gets rid of toxins and strengthens, regulates and rejuvenates the liver. It increases the liver's ability to break down toxins, hormones and provides long-term health benefits. Animal protein makes your liver work extra hard. So help your liver with a regular cleanse or avoiding those foods altogether. Two or three-day water or juice fast is a great way of giving your liver a break to allow it time to recuperate and repair itself. Remember to always do a colon cleanse first so the bowel can be in good working order and have a clear pathway to eliminate the toxins and waste. You can also take wheatgrass juice daily to help stimulate and heal your liver.

The Kidneys

The kidneys have a couple of different functions. The main purpose of the kidney is to separate urea, mineral salts, toxins, and other waste products from the blood. The kidneys also conserve water, salts, and electrolytes.

At least one kidney must function properly for life to be maintained, although the optimum would be with both kidneys, plus we have two kidneys for a good reason. The kidneys as a result of the cleansing process release toxins from the tissues into the blood.

The liver neutralises the toxins and sends them to the kidneys via the blood, and next the kidneys filter the blood and flush the toxins out of the body through the ureters, bladder and the urethra.

It's important for the kidneys and urinary system to be in excellent working condition because the cleansing process sends a lot of toxins for the kidneys to filter out. So cleansing the kidneys assists the process. It has been thought that kidney stones are formed from excess calcium, but I found through my research that it's mainly because of dehydration that allows waste to bind together forming stones. Drinking adequate water will help in proper blood circulation; when your blood is healthy, oxygen rich and flowing freely, your kidneys should also be healthy.

The Digestive System

This is just a short description of how the digestive system works. The digestive system is mainly one long tube going from the mouth down to the anus, it's made up of the digestive tract and a series of other organs that help the body break down and absorb food.

Organs that make up the digestive tract are the mouth, oesophagus, stomach, small intestine, large intestine also called the colon, rectum, and anus. Inside these organs is a lining called the mucosa. In the mouth, stomach, and small intestine, the mucosa contains tiny glands that produce juices to help digest food.

The digestive tract also contains a layer of smooth muscle that helps break down food and move it along the tract. The two digestive organs, the liver and the pancreas, produce digestive juices that reach the intestine through small tubes called ducts. The gallbladder stores the liver's digestive juices until they are needed in the intestine. Parts of the nervous and circulatory systems also play major roles in the digestive system.

When we eat, the food is not yet in a form that the body can use as nourishment. Food and drink must be changed into smaller molecules of nutrients before they can be absorbed into the blood and carried to cells throughout the body. Digestion is the process by which everything you eat and drink is broken down into their smallest parts so the body can use them to build and nourish cells and provide your body energy.

Digestion involves mixing food with digestive juices, moving it through the digestive tract and breaking down large molecules of food into smaller molecules. Digestion begins in the mouth. When you chew and swallow, the food goes through the digestive process and is completed in the small intestine. To help your digestion, make sure you chew your food slowly and thoroughly.

The waste products of this process include undigested parts of the food, such as fibre, and older cells that have been shed from the mucosa. These materials are meant to be pushed into the colon, where they remain until the faeces are expelled through a bowel movement.

Conditions of the Bowel

There is an increase in bowel conditions because of an impaired digestive system from the wrong type of foods that the body finds difficult to digest. This causes accumulation of human waste that should be expelled on a daily basis.

People that do not have a regular daily bowel movement are in danger of more serious bowel conditions. We have already mentioned earlier the importance of a regular daily bowel movement; when this does not happen, it may be the reason so many people have increasing bowel and colon cancer problems nowadays.

Some of the conditions of the bowel are:

Poor digestion, gas, bloating, flatulence, IBS (irritable bowel syndrome), piles, varicose veins, ulcers, genital warts, colitis, Crohn's disease and colon cancer.

IBS can lead to colitis and then to Crohn's disease if left untreated. IBS is excess mucus from the wrong types of food that causes the area to become sore and inflamed. It's irritation of the bowel lining or inflammation of the bowel, and this causes parasites to breed there.

To get rid of parasites, you should do a complete colon cleanse using cleansing foods and a gentle colon cleanser such as an oxygen or a gentle herbal colon cleanse including a liver and gallbladder cleanse, and a parasite cleanse. Then, take good bacteria such as probiotics, and this will keep parasites under control. Parasites are found mainly in the large intestines but parasites can also be found in the blood, brain and other organs of the body.

The bowels begin to be eaten away causing Crohn's disease. Dairy products trigger Crohn's disease, and with colitis and Crohn's, you will often find blood in the stool. Taking wheatgrass juice will help the area to heal. Green leafy vegetables and wheatgrass juice also stimulates and heals the liver.
And remember that regular internal cleansing and detox will keep parasites at bay. Conditions such as sciatica usually occur when excess human waste is pushed down on the nerve endings so you may get some relief from doing a colon cleanse. Please seek the advice of a good naturopath if you have a bowel condition.

Ways to avoid digestion problems

1. Eat fibrous foods such as fruits and vegetables that will aid digestion
2. Avoid processed foods that lead to digestive problems
3. Chew your food properly and thoroughly before swallowing
4. Don't talk and chew at the same time, as you also take in air
5. Don't drink and eat at the same time, as it dilutes the acids used for digestion
6. Try to get rid of stress and tension as this can cause constipation
7. Regularly cleanse and detoxify the colon area.
8. Stay hydrated
9. Taking digestive enzymes and probiotics can help

You can take flaxseed tea half an hour before each meal to coat the stomach lining. Flaxseed oil, which is an essential oil that can be taken daily, helps with lubrication and moves the bowels.
Eating and drinking at the same time causes you to become bloated, and before the body can break down the food it has to get rid of all the liquid first, and this can also give you gas. It's best to drink about 20 minutes before your meal, but this may take some getting used to because most people are accustomed to eating and drinking at the same time. Too much gravy on food can also dilute the nutrients from your vegetables.

Stress brings tension in the body. Tension will shut down the immune system and slow down the digestion. Constipation can also be a sign of extreme tension and stress.

As we get older, we lose the ability to make digestive enzymes, so you can get bloated. You may benefit from taking digestive enzymes with every meal, and these can be purchased from the health food shop. Digestive enzymes help to maintain a healthy intestinal lining and can be taken for some time until the system is fully healed.

Good bacteria can be taken in the form of probiotics or foods such as sauerkraut or kefir. Some forms of bacteria can cause disease so the idea of swallowing bacteria each day for your health might seem difficult to get used to at first. But a growing amount of scientific evidence suggests that you can treat and even prevent some illnesses with foods and supplements containing certain kinds of live bacteria. These can also be found in a health food shop, not the liquid milk type from the supermarket.
The wrong combination of foods will also make you bloated and sleepy, this also happens when you eat too much food. Most people do not know that the original size of their stomach is only the size of their fist, so the size of your fist is the natural amount of food that you should be eating, but our stomachs have stretched

over the years because of the amount of food we eat so are able to take in more food. To reduce bloating and other problems, you should eat no more than three or four types of foods at the same time. Try not to mix meat with grains because the body cannot break this combination down.

Although it's a typical way of eating, try to avoid eating meat together with starches such as rice and potatoes as this is very heavy on the digestive system.

Chewing gum on an empty stomach gives an illusion of food in the mouth; digestive acids are then released and burn the stomach lining, which can cause ulcers. It is better to chew the gum after a meal; this will release more acids to help digest your food. Make sure it's a natural, sugar-free healthy gum.

If you see black stool, it's either old stool or there could be blood in the stool, so make sure you keep an eye on things, so they don't escalate into further problems. You may want to get it checked out if it persists. As a result of eating processed and greasy foods accompanied with bad digestion the villi in the lower intestine responsible for absorbing the nutrients from our food becomes impaired, gets covered with mucus and cannot do its job.

Processed foods dump fats into the blood, the fat is picked up by the blood, from the villi, the blood is slowed down with the fat, and it sets, becomes thick and causes the blood to stagnate. This will cause conditions such as fibroids, endometriosis, ovarian cysts, blood clots, thrombosis and prostate problems.

The kidneys work very hard to clean the blood. Stagnation can also cause water retention, swollen ankles and red or darkened complexion.

People with high sugar levels often have dark circles under their eyes, this is a sign of liver and kidney weakness; you may feel a shortness of breath as water gets into the lungs, you then get high blood pressure because the kidney is slowing down and cannot get rid of the water as it becomes weaker because there is too much fat in the blood.

Puffiness under the eyes and sunken eyes in the morning can also be a sign of severe dehydration.

Everybody has Parasites

It sounds disgusting to think that we have living moving parasites inside us, but it's true everybody has them. No one wants to think that tiny bugs and worms could be using their body as a food supply while they breed by the millions in their intestine and bloodstream.

But parasites are a reality and more common than you realise. It's not a subject many like to discuss, and most people don't even realise that they have them. You are more likely to have them if you eat meat and sushi. Fortunately, you can get rid of most of them by doing a regular colon cleanse.
Dr Valerie Saxion ND is an expert on parasites, and below she talks extensively about the subject.

What is a parasite and what does it do?

A parasite is an organism that lives off the host, the host being you or I. A parasite eats, lays eggs and secretes waste.

How can a parasite possibly live in my body, and I don't even know it is there? The answer to this is simple. The purpose of a parasite is not to make itself known.

How can a parasite exist in the body without making its presence known?
If you know how to read the body and how to interpret its signals, then the presence of a parasite can be determined quite easily. Medical testing procedures only catch about 20%. Some parasites love sugar. If you are a person who craves sugar, you may have a sugar-loving parasite. In fact, parasites are known to be one of the causes of diabetic tendencies and blood sugar discrepancies.

Other parasites actually get their nutrition directly from the cells. Parasites eat your nutrients before you do! They get the best nutrients, and you get the scraps and leftovers. They grow healthy and fat, yet your organs and skin starve for nutrition.

Parasites can remain in your body for 10, 20, 30 years and more. In 1979, a British study reported on 600 former prisoners from World War II. These men had been stationed in the Far East. Thirty years after the war, 15% were still infected with a parasite called Strongyloides that they had contracted during the war. This means you could have eaten meat 10 years ago that was contaminated and still be hosting the tapeworms or other types of parasites that were in that meat.
Parasites can get into joints and eat the calcium linings of your bones. This can lead to arthritic tendencies. They can also eat the protein coating on the nerves, and this can cause a disruption in the nerve signals from the brain. One type of tiny parasite, which infects the colon, is called Entamoeba Histolytica. This type of infection can also be found in the liver, the lungs, and the brain. The disease is called amebiasis and is often transmitted via contaminated food or water.

Simply put, the secretions from parasites in our bodies are poisons and toxins that our bodies are forced to deal with by increasing the process of detoxification. Anyone who has experienced food poisoning or dysentery will tell you how debilitating these toxins can be.

Chronic parasitic infection secreting low levels of toxins can create an extremely stressed immune system. If parasites secrete toxins into our bodies that the bodies don't have time to neutralise, and we happen to be one of those people who drinks alcohol, smokes cigarettes, eats junk food and breathes polluted air, the extra stress and strain on the body's cleansing system can be enough to push the body into what we call toxic overload.

Toxic overload occurs when the four cleansing systems of the body have been pushed too far by an overload of toxins in the body. Parasite toxins in the body are one more thing a toxic body does not need. There are four cleansing systems of the body: the lungs, kidneys, skin and bowels.

If you find all this information about parasites cause for despair, take heart — there is a light at the end of the tunnel.

WHERE DO THEY COME FROM

Parasites come from many places, including use of hot tubs, hot springs, immigration, jet travel and a general decline of health in the modern world. Parasites also come from our inabilities to fight infections. Autoimmune disorders are ripe with parasitic infections.

Pick up any animal magazine and find advertisements for powerful medicines to rid house and farm animals of parasites. An alarming number of these, like liver flukes, giardia, trichinosis, roundworms, tapeworms, hookworms, pinworms and others are easily transferred to humans through contact with the animal's mouth parts, tongues, skin and through the eating of meat that has been either improperly handled or cooked.

In fact, humans play host to dozens of different parasites. Fish and seafood (especially Sushi) is another common way to contract parasites. More and more reports about infected drinking water are being published. Parasites can be the agents of death in elderly and weakened people when they drink such water.

Microscopic parasites can pass through even the most advanced filtering system; even the chemicals, which we are using against them, can't be effective in killing all of the parasites. Drinking water, swimming pools, and hot tubs are all breeding grounds for certain types of parasites. It is best to avoid all public pools and hot tubs.

There's much more information in "Every Body Has Parasites" by Valerie Saxion, N.D.

THINGS YOU CAN DO TO PROTECT AND CLEANSE YOUR SYSTEM

The distressing thing about parasites is that if you do get rid of them, you can easily be re-infected. Married couples tend to have them together.

Another method of detecting parasites is by YOUR symptom picture, just analysing how a person feels. But, because the symptom picture is so wide and varied, many other things can cause the same symptoms.

Colonics. Parasites thrive and breed in a cesspool. So what we must also do is remove the cesspool. How do we do that?

We need to ensure proper bowel function. Only a properly functioning digestive system can remove the cesspool. We should be eliminating at least one time a day, if not two or three times a day.

We spend more time, effort and money to see that our pets don't have parasites than we spend on ourselves. Yet when we think about it, isn't it important that we should be cleansing ourselves from the inside out?

The following points are important to remember:

Reduce the intake of processed and refined foods. You need to watch the white flour and the white sugar, reduce animal protein intake, reduce the coffee, cokes, all those things, which everybody knows. Now I am giving you a reason to do it. Also, increase the intake of 'living' foods, raw food, foods that have vitality such as fruits and vegetables, and whole grains. Why? Because these have the enzymes and the vitamins that our bodies desperately need in order to maintain them and run properly.

Also we need to supplement with a natural multivitamin and liquid mineral or a super food product so that we can repay the debts that we have created during the years when we were eating foods that were missing the nutrients that we needed.

Cleanse your body of parasites through a specific herbal parasite remedy. Now more than ever, I suggest doing a Parasite Cleanse. It's simply good health.

Fasting

Besides spiritual reasons for fasting, fasting is also a great way of giving your organs a break so that they can have time to repair themselves and heal. Fasting also has other benefits such as giving you a clearer, fresher complexion, removing fogginess of the brain and helping you to think more clearly and making clearer and more positive decisions.

If I were given a diagnosis of a chronic condition, the first thing I would do is to stop eating and go on a fast to cleanse my system and give my system a break so it could start to repair itself and heal. I would not put any food in my system for a few days, I would just drink good clean, pure structured living water for a few days, after this I would continue on a juice fast of mainly organic vegetable juices, maybe adding an apple to make it palatable.

I would not eat any processed foods, sugary foods or fatty foods but concentrate on giving my body the correct natural whole plant-based foods that were designed for my body as fuel, in its most raw and organic natural state as possible. I would not be thinking about costs at this stage; I would re-adjust my budget to make sure I was putting living natural organic foods into my system at this stage because my health is more important.

A fast can also consist of having just salads for a few days, remember that salad dressing can be fattening so you can use lemon or apple cider vinegar (the cloudy type) and virgin cold-pressed olive oil and a drop of natural organic honey as a dressing or make your own low fat dressing. Juicing is also a great fast that you can do, but the best type of fasting is water fasts where you eat no food but only drink water for a few days. But don't start with this type of fasting if you've never fasted before. Start with salads or juicing.

One of the quickest way of healing is doing a complete water fast, this has to be done with good pure water, but again it is very important to consult someone who is an expert or has good experience in this field and knows what they are doing so it's done with supervision, especially if you plan to do it for a longer period.

Three phases of sickness

Having been sick myself and raised out of the sickness industry, I have been through three phases of sickness. I started off in phase three as a teenager and due to the fact that I did not know any better and was too sick to do anything about it. From there I was almost pulled into phase two but refused to be in that situation for the rest of my life. I finally found myself in phase one where I healed myself when I became tired of being sick.

Phase 1

Sick and on medication for a while; I was getting worse and not getting better with the medication and was desperate to come off tablets and fed up of being drugged up to my eyeballs when in hospital. I was sick and tired of being sick. Although I did not initially know what to do about it, I began to actively search for ways to get better. I took advice on natural remedies and was open to trying other alternative methods to see if they work. My search finally paid off when I found natural alternatives that helped my situation.

Phase 2

I got a lot of attention because of my illness. I was entitled to various types of benefits, although I found this very helpful, I felt trapped and became dependant. There is no judgment here on those that are in this situation, but you can find freedom and get out of it if you are determined.

I was desperate to get well so I could find work to support myself. It was very difficult to let go of everything that came as a result of the illness, but most people with sickle that I know, often try to find work when they are well, but then cannot hold the job down because they get sick again so frequently, so I remained sick and would have been on medication for the rest of my life, but I was determined to come out of it. But at one point I felt as if I have no choice because I was too sick to do anything about it.

Phase 3
Being born with a hereditary condition, I thought it was just bad luck so I was not originally open to research to see how I can help myself to get better, I did not even know this was possible as I though the doctor's word was final. I believed that the doctor and the hospital know best and are the only way.

I put my health and life completely in the hands of the doctor and hospital because I thought that is the only way to go when you are sick, based on what I was taught. Because I was not getting better, I accepted my situation for a while and believed that was it and I had to remain on drugs for the rest of my life. This is where the majority are at.

Drugs simply put a plaster on the symptoms, they don't address or attempt to resolve the cause, and worse can produce life-threatening side effects.
The question remains: Why take dangerous drugs when you can use nutrients from living foods that both deal with the root cause and help alleviate the symptoms? Again, it's a lack of knowledge. We do not have to accept or live with our conditions. It's not about just managing your condition with drugs, but the goal should be to get your life back and to be completely healed and free of sickness.

CHAPTER 12

Cleanse Your Way To Health
Internal Body Cleansing

Internal cleansing of whole body is one of the biggest missing elements of our health that is critical for the proper functioning of every organ and cell in our body.

Today's typical diet is deficient and consists of foods that are high in preservatives and fatty substances that harm the body as we have seen. Most of our supermarket foods are processed.

Eating processed and convenient foods comes at a price, and we see with today's statistics of chronic disease that many are paying the price with their health and even their lives.

Our bodies need help to detoxify and clean our system by way of internal body cleansing. Let us find out about the facts of Internal Body Cleansing.

As we mentioned before, our body was designed to clean itself internally, naturally through certain organs like the liver and kidneys whilst eating the original diet (natural whole foods, fruits, vegetables, herbs and clean pure water) that are cleansing to the body.

Because we live in a toxic environment and suffering the consequences of our modern diet, our body is no longer capable of self-cleansing internally without the correct foods and herbs.

The most important thing when cleansing is that you find a cleansing program that is mild and provides an easy way to cleanse the body and the blood of impurities while at the same time feeding it with the highest grade of nutrients. If you have a chronic condition, you may want to start with cleansing foods then move on to cleansing products as you gain more strength.

When you do an internal body cleanse, you will not only have a cleaner system, but don't be surprised if you lose weight, have proper functioning organs, see a reversal of minor and chronic conditions, notice healthier skin, hair, nails and brighter eyes. You may also notice more energy and vitality. And remember the possible detox effect mentioned earlier. Just drink more water to flush the toxins out of your system quicker or start slowly by eliminating one bad food at a time.

Oestrogen dominance and associated health problems

Oestrogen is a female hormone; oestrogen and progesterone are essential to the health of every woman. These two hormones exist in a delicate balance, and when that balance is thrown off, various health complications can occur. From puberty through the childbearing years, there is supposed to be a delicate balance between oestrogen and progesterone.

The amount of these hormones produced by the body can vary from month-to-month and year-to-year depending on many factors, including stress, nutrition and exercise. Although oestrogen is best known as a female hormone, the male body naturally produces it in small amounts.

Oestrogen dominance, on the other hand, affects both men and women and is caused by Xenoestrogens into our environment.

These are chemically manufactured oestrogen that mimic oestrogen. Our food supply is saturated with them. Products such as pesticides and animal growth hormones used on the farm are good examples.

These substances are causing a lot of problems to the reproductive system of women as well as men. Some women that have a toxic overload of these substances are finding it very difficult to conceive. Men are also having problems with issues such as lower sperm counts and problems with erectile dysfunction. The key is to avoid using foods and products that contain these substances and do periodic cleansing to make sure the substances do not remain in your body but are cleansed out.

Ever wonder why young girls are starting their periods earlier, some as young as nine and ten years old, and developing physically and sexually much quicker? That's Xenoestrogens at work.

Symptoms that can occur from oestrogen dominance

Irregular menstrual flow; cramping
Bloating; depression; irritability
Migraine headaches; insomnia; epilepsy
Miscarriages; infertility; incontinence; endometriosis
Hot flashes; night sweats; vaginal dryness
Hypoglycaemia; chronic fatigue syndrome; yeast infections
Heart palpitations and other cardiovascular disorders
Early bone loss pre-menopause, osteoporosis.

See below a list of more Xenoestrogens to avoid.

Xenoestrogens contributes to "excess oestrogen" or "oestrogen dominance."

The short answer is to go as organic and "green" as you can.

Avoid:
* Commercially raised, non-organic meats such as beef, chicken, and pork
* Commercial dairy products including milk, butter, cheese, and ice cream. Use only organic products that do not contain bovine growth hormone
* Unfiltered water, including water you bath in, use filtered water and shower head filters * Laundry detergent, use a non-chemical detergent
* Dryer sheets and fabric softeners, use a non-chemical brand
* Avoid Birth Control Pills.
* Hormone replacement therapy (HRT)
* Progesterone creams with parabens and other preservatives
* Unfermented Soy and Processed Soy products
* Avoid sunflower oil, cottonseed oil and canola oil
Use olive oil or coconut oil
* Avoid coffee and caffeine
* Do not use shampoos, lotions, soap and cosmetics that contain parabens or phenoxyethanol, almost all contain them, these chemicals go through your skin and into the blood
* Shampoos that purposely include oestrogen (these are shampoos that cater to the African-American market)
* Avoid reheating foods in plastic or Styrofoam containers
* Avoid drinking out of plastic cups and containers
* Air fresheners that contain phthalates
* Avoid naturally occurring plant oestrogens:
* 4-Methylbenzylidene camphor (4-MBC) (sunscreen lotions)
* Butylated hydroxyanisole / BHA (food preservative)
* Atrazine (weed killer)
* Bisphenol A (monomer for polycarbonate plastic and epoxy resin; antioxidant in plasticisers)
* Dieldrin (insecticide)
* DDT (insecticide)

* Endosulfan (insecticide)
* Erythrosine / FD&C Red No. 3
* Heptachlor (insecticide)
* Lindane / hexachlorocyclohexane (insecticide)
* Methoxychlor (insecticide)
* Nonylphenol and derivatives (industrial surfactants; emulsifiers for emulsion polymerisation; laboratory detergents; pesticides)
* Polychlorinated biphenyls / PCBs (in electrical oils, lubricants, adhesives, paints)
* Parabens (lotions)
* Phenosulfothiazine (a red dye)
* Phthalates (plasticisers)
* DEHP (plasticiser for PVC)

Other Ways to Avoid Oestrogen Dominance

Maintain a healthy weight. Oestrogen is produced by fat cells, so one of the most common causes of oestrogen dominance in both men and women is obesity.

Drink 6-8 glasses of water daily. Staying hydrated helps maintain kidney function and encourage healthy hormone balance.

Eat a diet high in fibre because it binds to excess oestrogen and removes it from the body as waste.   It also helps prevent constipation, which exacerbates oestrogen dominance.

Avoid hormone-injected meat and chicken that contains high levels of man-made oestrogen and will throw your hormones out of balance.

Exercise regularly. Regular exercise promotes healthy hormone balance.

If you drink alcohol, drink in moderation, or not at all. Alcohol is an "estrogenic" substance, meaning it causes the body to produce more oestrogen. It also interferes with the kidneys' ability to remove excessive oestrogen from the body. Alcoholism is another common cause of oestrogen dominance in men. (**Source: health science**)

Toxic Thinking and Emotions

Toxic thoughts and emotions are also a contributing factor to sickness and disease. Studies show that a negative thought could deplete your immune system and eventually eat away at your health like cancer.

You are what you think and believe, and what you think and believe is usually what manifests itself in your life.
Dr Caroline Leaf has studied the effects of toxic thinking and emotions on the brain and has discovered that emotions such as:

Anger, hate, bitterness, unforgiveness, rejection, and negative thoughts cause toxic thinking in the brain that can eventually affect your physical body. This is what you call a fear-based emotion that picks up the wrong type of chemicals in your brain and puts stress in your body that produces a physical reaction in your body.

This affects you intellectually, emotionally and physically, manifesting in sickness because of a depleted immune system from a lack of nutrition.
Medical research has shown that these toxic thoughts and emotions can actually be seen on an image of your brain in the form of thorns or branches that spread, but as you take control of your thought life and make decisions using your heart rather than your mind, the thorns actually drop off giving you a calmer feeling of peace.

Dr Leaf's book is, Who Switched off My Brain?

CHAPTER 13

Anti-ageing and Weight Loss

Aging slowly is possible.

Ageing is something that the majority of people if not everyone except for children are concerned about. Why do some people age very slowly and look much younger than their age while the majority of people look their age or older? It doesn't seem fair, does it? We have heard that this is all under the control of our genes, and that might be true to some extent but not all.

The ageing process depends on a combination of both genetic and environmental factors; as mentioned earlier, we are told that genetics amounts to only around 10%. Recognising that every individual has his or her own unique genetic makeup and environment, which interact with each other, helps us understand why the ageing process can occur at such different rates in different people.

A lot of people do not realise that they are rapidly contributing to the acceleration of their ageing process by their day-to-day activity. Anti-ageing treatments are big business and a multi-billion industry. There are many treatments out there dealing with the superficial problems of the external skin. But healing starts from within.

If your body is in balance and functioning correctly from correct minerals and nutrition, you will have proper blood circulation and oxygenation, faster cell renewal, your eliminating organs will be in good working order, your cells will be nourished and it will automatically show on your skin. So when thinking about anti-ageing treatments, remember that beauty starts from within. Make sure you start internally with the cleansing and nutrition, because sometimes that's all it takes for you to start seeing the difference.

It has been said that the process of ageing for everybody starts with oxidation. Oxidation, to put it simply, is a process by which oxygen causes rust on metal. Some examples of oxidation are an apple cut in half turning brown, a rusty nail, or a copper coin turning green.

A similar process takes place in your cells. Oxidants, commonly known as free radicals attacking your cells causes them to age and decay. We see the outward effect of this process in the skin becoming wrinkled. Researchers have found that oxidative free radicals contribute to ailments such as cataracts, arthritis and other ailments associated with ageing.

You can combat the destructive effects of oxidants becoming free and radical with antioxidants that pacify the free radicals and limit their attack.

Within the human body, millions of processes are occurring at all times. These processes require oxygen. Unfortunately, that same life giving oxygen can create harmful side effects, or oxidant substances, which cause cell damage unless it's activated stabilised oxygen, then the benefits can be amazing
as I have experienced.

Eating a diet rich in plenty of antioxidants such as berries will reduce free radical damage.

Secrets to Real Weight Loss and fat burning without calorie counting

There is a lot of contradicting and confusing information out there regarding weight loss and diets, but the real information often gets lost in all the confusion and misinformation

It can become very overwhelming with thousands of diets, weight loss pills and calorie counting programs. You're doing everything you know but still end up with the weight on your body. So to make sure you lose the weight that you need to, where do you start? First of all, diets do not work, especially if you are still eating processed, fatty and sugary foods because these are the culprits. There are four basic principles you need to know and do.

1. You need to do an internal overhaul to cleanse all the excess waste, backed up human waste, excess mucus and toxins that are clogging up your system, including your liver that is meant to break down the fat and filter harmful substances from the blood. If you're eating certain harmful foods, your liver is working hard at filtering these substances from the blood and cannot effectively break down the fats that are meant to be broken down. So cleansing will make sure your liver and other organs are working properly to help you get rid of unwanted fat. You will be shocked at the amount of weight you lose just through cleansing alone.

2. You need to eat more natural raw living foods to reduce fat from your body, as well as eating natural good fats such as flaxseed oil, hemp oil, olive oil and coconut oil that will assist in the fat burning process contrary to what you may have heard. There has been a lot of misinformation regarding coconut oil in the past, but there is now plenty of good information regarding the amazing benefits of coconut oil and other good fats that actually help to burn fat. Healthy fats are essential for many functions of the body; it's the bad saturated fats you need to avoid.

196

3. You need to know the foods that are preventing you from burning fat. Many of these processed, fatty and sugary foods are advertised as healthy foods. The foods on the dangerous foods list are typical of the foods that will put weight on you fast and prevent you from losing weight and burning the excess fat.

4. You need to watch your sugar levels. When your sugar levels are constantly between 100-120, your body releases insulin, insulin signals your body to store fat, and that is the complete opposite of what you want. Remember in point 1 that if your liver is working hard to filter all the harmful substances you put in your body, it cannot effectively break down the fat as it's supposed to. When your insulin levels are high, they can also go down to an extreme low, and this is where you start to get hungry and start to crave for unhealthy foods. Regulate your insulin levels by avoiding artificial sugars, processed foods and foods made from white flour products as they all turn to sugar in the body and interfere with insulin levels. Eat more natural plant-based vegan foods that will balance your blood sugar.

Summarise on weight loss

1. Internal body cleanse – cleanse the whole system of excess waste, mucus and toxins including the bowels, liver, kidney and bladder, lungs, and rid the body of excess mucus and parasites. You also need heavy metal detox and hormone balance by eating natural foods or natural supplements that will balance your hormones.

2. Again, stay away from the dangerous foods listed in this book
3. Eat an 80% raw food diet and 20% cooked. Works quicker on a complete raw diet.

197

4. Avoid labelled so called diet foods and drinks. Check the ingredient for sugar and saturated fat content. Especially artificial sugars.

5. Exercise regularly, get the body moving

Avoid the bad fats such as saturated fats, hydrogenated fats, vegetable oils and all other oils except for the good oils such as natural oils found in avocado and nuts, extra virgin cold pressed olive oil, flaxseed oil, hemp oil, coconut oil. If you can do this, it will not be too difficult to burn the fat and lose the weight permanently.

6. Be sure to keep a daily journal by recording your current weight and measurements, taking your measurements as you go along. This will encourage you to continue as you start to see the weight coming off.

Taking measurements is more important than getting on a weighing scale because as you exercise daily you will build muscle that can look like you are gaining weight, but you are actually just gaining muscle, but you will see through taking actual body measurements that you are losing the weight.

How To Heal Your Face Naturally

Many people are dissatisfied with their face; it may no longer have the youthful glow and plumpness.
Blemishes, wrinkles, spots, moles, pimple, line and creases are a sign not only of your external face but also a sign of what is going on in your body. They did not just appear on your face. Over the years, we watch the skin on our face and body gravitate in the direction of our feet. There are many causes for this including nutritional deficiency. But what a lot of people seem to neglect is the fact that if you do not exercise your muscles, not only in your body but your face also, it will soon start to show years faster than if you exercise the muscles of your face with daily facial exercises. You can dramatically slow down the sagging of the face making it taut and trim and even reverse the sagging.

Although I am ageing very slowly because of my nutritional intake and do not have any problems with drooping skin and muscles on my face, I started to do facial exercises about one year ago, and I must say that there has been a vast improvement in how my face has become more taut, it's almost like it's reverting back to when I was in my 20s. I am extremely excited about this discovery.

There are two sets of facial exercises I do. I do one set for a few weeks and then I alternate and do the other. The first is by Carol Maggio, she came up with Facercise, you can find her clips on the internet and her DVDs are also available to purchase.

The second set of facial exercises is by Pete from Renew me. She came up with Facerobics. You can find lots of her free clips on her Renew me site or on the internet.
They are both perfect examples of what they promote. You can see the youthfulness on their faces, despite their ages.

Causes Of Accelerated Ageing

Free Radical damage

Bad nutrition (processed, fatty and sugary foods)

Lack of vitamins and minerals

Too many cooked foods and not enough raw enzyme rich foods

Dehydration

Too much alcohol

Smoking and taking recreational drugs

Pharmaceutical drugs

Lack of sleep

Putting toxins in your system

Harsh chemical skin care

Negative thinking and speaking

Stress

My tips for slowing down the ageing process

- **Secret No. 1** Raw natural electric foods, fruits, raw vegetables, sprouted seed (Living whole foods) because beauty starts from within.
- **Secret No. 2** Regular detox and deep cleansing of the internal organs to regulate bowels.
- **Secret No. 3** Activated Stabilised Oxygen cleanses and rebuilds, when the cells are clean, and blood purified, this improves the skin, allowing it to repair itself from the inside out. You will begin to see a huge improvement in

your skin externally as well as improvement to hair and nails.

- **Secret No. 4** Facial exercises, if you want to avoid a sagging body and achieve a toned and fit body, you can engage in a specific exercise program to help achieve your goals. The face is no different from the body in that respect; you can practice daily facial exercises to plump up, reduce wrinkles and improve your skin overall.

Other Tips for slowing down the ageing process

- Hydration, at least 6-8 glasses of good, pure clean living water per day.
- Glutathione, which is found naturally in the body is the body's first defence against anti-ageing and toxins. Different circumstances cause our glutathione levels to deplete, so the body rapidly begins to deteriorate. The best glutathione supplement would be one that activates and increases your body's own glutathione levels.
- Lots of antioxidant found in fruits mainly berries, Vitamin A, C & E.
- 7-8 hours of sleep
- Going to bed early 10-11 rather than late will help your body to repair and renew
- Resveratrol found in the skin of red grapes can be bought as a supplement.
- CoQ 10 helps to repair and restore the skin while sleeping
- Get stress out of your body
- Use gentle natural or organic skin care
- Exfoliating skin using a natural gentle exfoliate once a week to remove dead skin. I sometimes use bicarbonate of soda on a wet face, massaging it in with my fingers, then I rinse off and tone using diluted apple cider vinegar.

- Wash face with filtered or natural mineral water, rather than chlorinated tap water
- Apply a clay facemask once or twice a month.
- Always use upward strokes when moisturising face or body as this goes against gravity and will also slow down sagging of the skin.
- I keep my skin silky smooth by using raw coconut oil or Shea butter as an all over moisturiser and cleanser and then tone with diluted apple cider vinegar mixed with water. There are plenty of other natural face cleansing regimes you can find, I'd just make sure they are natural and contain no chemicals.
- Telomeres. I recently learnt about telomers in relation to slowing down the ageing process by Dr Al Sears. The longer your telomere, the slower you age and the shorter they are, the faster you age. Do a bit of research on this as he will explain it far better than I can, then you can see how it can benefit you.

Quick tips for maintaining perfect health

1. Oxygen - we need to oxygenate our body, as the chronic condition or disease will not be able to stay in a body that is oxygen rich.

Oxygen also allows the cells free capacity to build the cells the way they need to be built and strengthen the immune system to fight disease; extra oxygen can also purify your bloodstream, improve memory and help your body to repair injuries quicker. Exercise, relaxation, and slow deep breathing can help the body to get more oxygen rather than shallow breathing that robs the body of oxygen.

2. Hydration - of the system is also important as a lot of the foods we eat and the drinks we drink nowadays dehydrate the body. When you are thirsty, it's the body's final warning that you do not have enough hydration. If you have proper hydration, you will never or rarely get thirsty.

Your cells can burn out if you don't have enough hydration. Causing build up in the body that causes enzyme function to cease. Enzymes are important for maintaining life.

But don't overdo it on the water either. A litre should be ok for the average person. You may need more if you have very dry skin. Enzymes are important for maintaining life.

3. Exercise - movement of the body allows the body to act as a pump for the cellular structure, this allows the water to pump the body of toxins and excess mucus from the body; it also allows the blood to be pumped around the body to parts of the body that is not doing so well, exercise gets the lymphatic system moving so can promote healing.

4. Stress Reduction - keeping stress in the body will cause the body to hold on to accumulations that need to be eliminated from the body and will deplete the immune system so it cannot function properly to fight off disease. Meditation and exercise can be a great way of reducing stress.

5. Eliminate Toxins – It's important to eliminate toxins in the body because chronic conditions and diseases are a result of toxic overload in the body making the body acidic, so eliminating toxins, accumulated waste, heavy metals, radiation, etc. will also help to eliminate the disease. Cleansing the body will allow the system to remove the excess waste and toxins that have accumulated over time and will also allow the body to absorb the nutrients in the food. It is also important to eliminate any toxins and chemicals found in personal care products and home cleaning products.

6. Diet and Nutrition – Eating a lighter nutritious diet, not too much food, but for perfect health, it is especially important to have the greater percentage of raw living foods in your diet. There is no rule that you have to eat three meals a day, it's just tradition; the people that live the longest eat only one or two meals a day. Eat mainly vegetables in their most raw state and fruit as these foods contain plenty of water that will also hydrate your body. They contain oxygen that will help oxygenate your body; they are chlorophyll and antioxidants that will oxygenate your body and remove free radical damage. The body will have sufficient nutrients from eating these living foods so will feel more satisfied and less hungry, so that you will require less food.

Conclusion

To conclude, I am just going to summarise the information in the book as a reference and guide to the causes, and the solutions you can take to prevent as well as reverse sickness, get well and stay well, lose stubborn fat and slow down the ageing process. Remember that the biggest secret is simple common sense and your own research to discover what works best with your body.

- We saw the reason why many people are getting sick and why chronic disease is increasing at an alarming rate each year is because of the problem of accumulation, lack of proper blood circulation and a deficiency of essential vitamins, minerals, nutrients and dead foods void of the living enzymes that the body needs as the correct fuel in order to function correctly.

- We discovered that accumulation, lack of circulation and deficiency that happens as a result of what we eat and drink on a daily basis, as well as the toxins we ingest from various chemicals in our food, skincare, and home products as well as stress, are a big cause for illness.

- We learnt that the body was designed to function in a certain way, and when we do not give the body what it needs to function in that way, it leads to the cells, organs and body breaking down and eventually getting sick, or leads to premature death.

- We discovered the solution was cleansing the body of accumulated waste and giving the body what it needs so the body can do what it's supposed to do, and that's to heal itself naturally. This is how you can reverse your condition — give your body the correct building blocks it needs so it can heal itself naturally as it was designed to do.

- We learnt that the correct foods or fuel that were created for our body to function properly were live foods that contain living enzymes. We also learnt about dead foods, what they do to your body and how you can cleanse to reverse the effects of these foods that have accumulated in your system over the years.

- We learnt the importance of taking control of your own health as only you can do this. You are the only one that has your best interest at heart when it comes to your health.

Now that you know that you can prevent chronic conditions and even reverse them by cleansing the body and eating the correct living foods and getting the correct plant based vitamins and minerals into your body, you have no excuses.

Don't leave your health to chance, and don't live with your condition just because you have been told that there is nothing that can be done for you. In medical terms they may be right, there may be nothing left that they can do for you, but nutritionally it could be the beginning of the end of your condition. Don't give up.

There is always something you can do; there is always a way out of your situation. All you need to do is go back to the basics and create your health, go back to the beginning and start all over again. Start by doing the right things, and you will see a change in your health and life. If you do this and keep it up, there will be no need for you to ever get sick. Create your health, starting today.

"There are no incurable diseases just incurable people" - Dr R. Schulze

—

with more nutrients than any of the others. Most of the benefits of apples are found in the skin.

Berry Smoothie for antioxidants

Blackberries, Blueberries, Raspberries, Strawberries and coconut water, cream or coconut milk. (Optional) you can replace the coconut cream or milk with orange or apple juice.

This is the ultimate antioxidant smoothie. They are loaded with antioxidant power, protecting your body against inflammation, free radical damage and keep you looking younger. They also increase your lifespan. Berries are loaded with fibre, which helps you feel full.

Green Smoothie for alkalizing

Can be any combination of any green vegetables such as spinach, cucumber, kale, romaine lettuce, parsley, etc. You can juice them or put them in a blender and blend together adding a bit of water or apple or orange juice and banana.

The most nutritious of all is the green smoothie. Pure chlorophyll, the pigment part of the plant that gives it that green colour. Also known as the blood of the plant, and the most incredible thing is that its structure is very similar to the haemoglobin in the blood that carries oxygen. Chlorophyll has also been known to normalise blood counts. Prepare yourself for plenty of energy and even certain ailments disappearing if you continue with green smoothies or green juices. I often add ginger and turmeric to my smoothies.

Coconut Milk or Cream

Coconut cream bears the saturated fatty acid structure. However, the structure is in the form of medium-chain rather than those animal saturated fats, which are connected together as long-chain. Long-chain is extremely difficult to break down, and so it gets easily stored as fat. Medium-chain breaks down easily and converts to energy (like good carbohydrate) instantly. Coconut, through its lauric acid, converts to monolaurin (an antiviral, antibacterial and boosts your immune system and protects you against many viruses, including hepatitis C and herpes and has many other incredible benefits.

Lower Your Blood Sugar and Blood Pressure

Liquidise: Raw ginger, turmeric, parsley, watercress, avocado, lemon juice and apple juice or water preferably. Drink daily.
The above ingredients combined and liquidised will help you to reduce your blood sugar levels and will also get good circulation going.

Other options for Smoothies

For the best smoothies, you need to add either banana, mango, avocado or coconut cream to get that creamy and smooth texture.

Option 1. Fresh orange juice or water, banana, mango, beetroot and cucumber

Option 2. Fresh orange juice or water, avocado, banana and pineapple

Option 3. Fresh orange juice or water, banana, pineapple, celery and ginger

Option 4. Fresh apple juice or water, strawberries, banana and cucumber

Option 5. Peaches, orange juice or water, banana and kiwi

Walnuts
Flax seeds, tan and brown
Macadamia
Pecans
Pine Nuts
Pumpkin Seeds
Chia seeds
Sesame Seeds, tan and black
Sunflower Seeds

Oils and Nut Butters
Coconut oil
Extra Virgin Olive Oil
Flax Oil
Hemp Oil
Tahini

Dried Fruit
Cranberries
Goji Berries
Dates
Raisins

Seaweed (can be added to salads)
Dulse
Nori sheets
Wakame

Sweeteners
Date syrup
Sweet freedom
Natural maple syrup
Raw Agave Nectar
Stevia

Coconut palm sugar

Spices and salt
Sea salt
Basil, dried
Black Pepper
Cayenne, ground
Chili Powder
Cinnamon, ground
Curry Powder
Cumin Powder
Dill
Paprika
Sage
Tarragon
Thyme
Turmeric
Vanilla pod

Miscellaneous
Apple Cider Vinegar
Coconut Aminos
Tamari sauce
Balsamic Vinegar (use in moderation)
Carob (or Cocoa) Powder
Nutritional yeast (for thickening sauces and for cheesy flavours)

Disclaimer:

The author of this book is not a licensed medical professional. The information presented is not intended to diagnose or treat disease. The author makes no assurances of the data presented nor to the claims and information that are made by referenced documents or websites

WS - #0130 - 240122 - C72 - 210/148/17 - PB - 9781784562717 - Gloss Lamination